Spartan CEO

SIX PILLARS OF EXECUTIVE PERFORMANCE

To Brian from Moira 21/6/2020

Corrie Jonn Block, PhD, DBA

PASSIONPRENEUR
P U B L I S H I N G

Spartan CEO
Copyright © 2020 Corrie Jonn Block, PhD, DBA
First published in 2020

ISBN
Paperback: 978-0-6486663-8-7
E-book: 978-0-6486663-9-4

Because of the dynamic nature of the Internet, any web addresses or links contained in this book may have changed since publication and may no longer be valid. The information in this book is based on the author's experiences and opinions. The views expressed in this book are solely those of the author and do not necessarily reflect the views of the publisher; the publisher hereby disclaims any responsibility for them.

The author of this book does not dispense any form of medical, legal, financial, or technical advice either directly or indirectly. The intent of the author is solely to provide information of a general nature to help you in your quest for personal development and growth. In the event you use any of the information in this book, the author and the publisher assume no responsibility for your actions. If any form of expert assistance is required, the services of a competent professional should be sought.

Publishing information
Publishing, design, and production facilitated by
Passionpreneur Publishing
www.PassionpreneurPublishing.com

Melbourne, VIC | Australia

Dedication

For my beautiful wife and best friend, Nicole, who crashed into me during one of my darkest times, brought life and light to me, restored my faith in myself, and generously bound her destiny to mine. Thank you for your partnership, your quality of love, and for putting up with my shit. It's a dcuk!

Table of Contents

Foreword

by Joe De Sena, Founder and CEO, Spartan

Growing up, my mother was really into yoga and eating healthy at a time when it wasn't popular, especially in Queens. She introduced me to a whole world centered around mindful, healthy living, to the point where we even had a Buddhist monk living with us.

At the same time, I took the advice of a neighbor and I started cleaning pools, which taught me the true value of hard work, the importance of discipline and determination, and always going the extra mile. I parlayed my seven-hundred-client pool cleaning business into a construction company, fought my way into Cornell University, and I found myself on Wall Street—with a successful career, but at the cost of health and well-being.

The long hours, sitting at a desk, entertaining in the evening—it wasn't for me, and it shouldn't be for anybody. I was taking the stairs one day and happened to meet a man who was walking up and down with a dumbbell. He had fallen into the same routines I had, and turned things around. He told me I needed to sign up for a race, to put a date on the calendar. After following his advice, I never looked back. Soon after turning things around for myself, I knew that I had to help others, as he had helped me. So, I moved my family to Vermont and set out on my mission to transform lives, and Spartan was born.

Building the business to where it is today, was not an easy task. I tried and failed so many times before hitting the right concept in 2010—ten years after I began and just as my life savings was about to run out. It took discipline, determination, and more than anything else, the knowledge that I could do it, to start a brand and a movement that could change the world.

Spartan's culture is led by our mission to transform a hundred million lives. Everyone that works for us is here because they believe in that mission. As CEO, it's my job to motivate the team, and with a purpose as strong as ours, it's hard not to. I believe that to inspire others, you have to have a mission and a vision that is powerful, purposeful, and that you believe in. Everyone on the team is driven, has clear goals, and holds themselves and each other accountable, which is 100 percent necessary for growth.

I am leading by example and I could not be prouder of the team around me, who take that lead and drive the business forward. Sure, I wake up at 4:30 a.m. every morning, workout, then wake my kids up at five and work out with them. I carry a 40-pound kettlebell everywhere I go. Eat a plant-based diet, and I don't drink. While I don't expect all of my employees to be carbon copies of me, I know that what I do affects them. It drives a corporate culture that reflects our mission. We live healthily, work hard, and do not back down to obstacles that stand in our way.

If everyone in the company, and around the world takes steps and incorporates elements of what I consider "the Spartan way" into their daily routines, we'll all be healthier. So, as I work to inspire the company, and our seven-million strong community, I'm encouraged when I see our colleagues drinking green juice instead of soda or taking the stairs inside of the elevator; it's so encouraging. When I see our team and community doing this, I know it's only going to lead to others doing the same as well. It reinforces that our team is driven, loves what they do, and shares our mission.

I cannot stand to see a leader in business, a CEO, an entrepreneur, anybody who is crushing that part of their life, and does not take care of themselves. My father was an amazing entrepreneur, but he was different from my mother, he drank a ton of soda, ate a lot of junk food, and, that's not acceptable for a leader. Business leaders are supposed to be like athletes, we're expected to put our blood and sweat into our businesses, and that's hard. The only way to manage the stresses of the job and anything that may be weighing in from your personal life is to take care of yourself. Act like the athlete you need to be to succeed both in business and in your personal life.

There is a major opportunity right now, for business leaders to band together to learn and put into practice the ways in which to live a healthier lifestyle. It's imperative to keep our body and minds strong—more than that, it's a responsibility. By taking care of ourselves, we are setting a proven example that exercise and healthy living only have a positive effect on productivity. We owe that to our workforce, who will, in turn, be stronger and perform better.

As you read Spartan CEO, you will learn a lot of important ways in which to lead. Dr. Corrie Block brilliantly upholds my conviction that placing the health and well-being of yourself and the workforce above all else, is the foundation of a successful venture.

When we first started Spartan, our motto was, "You'll know at the finish line" and that rings true to this day. We founded Spartan to show people that the challenges they faced on the course, mimicked those that they faced in everyday life. By showing people that the human body is capable of things greater than the mind ever thought possible—and once that way of thinking takes shape—you gain the confidence needed to tackle anything that comes your way on and off the course, and that metaphor rings through the pages ahead.

Aroo!

Joe De Sena
Founder and CEO, Spartan

Introduction

This Is Sparta!

Do you remember the movie *300*? I do. The direction, the effects, the artistic coloring of the film, the drama, and dialogue. It is amazing. One of the best films I have ever seen and a massive leadership inspiration. I think everyone had a crush on Gerard Butler, including me. He was beautiful. The character of Leonidas was compelling, powerful, focused, and passionate. He was all of the things we think of when we think of great leaders, and his story is truly inspiring.

In 491 BCE, Darius the Great sent emissaries to convince the Spartans to accept Persian rule, but Sparta was a proud city with strong leaders. They tossed Darius's messengers into a well in protest, a powerful insult to Darius. A decade later, Darius's successor, Xerxes, returned to finish the job with more than 70,000 fighters. Hopelessly outnumbered, Leonidas, king of Sparta, gathered his best 300 warriors and went to meet the Persians at the Pass of Thermopylae.

There at the pass, a few-hundred-meter-wide gap allowed only a few of the Persians to advance at a time, rendering their massive numbers futile. Wave after wave of the Persian army crashed against the Spartan stones. For two days, the Spartans held back the Persians until Leonidas was betrayed by his fellow Greek, Ephialtes, who, in exchange for a position of power, informed Xerxes of an alternative route around the pass.

Xerxes sent some of his army along the bypass, led by Ephialtes himself, and collapsed the Spartans' only tactical advantage. Having lost the pass, Leonidas and his 300 continued to fight but were ultimately defeated on the third day of the battle.

Leonidas ruled Sparta from 490 to 480 BCE, a decade during a time when ancient Greece was steadily improving economically but was still very poor. In the fifth century BCE, Herodotus wrote, "Hellas has always had poverty as its companion" (Ober, 2015, p. 76). Leonidas died in August 480 BCE at the age of 60, only about a decade after becoming king. Keep in mind that he didn't die of natural causes but fighting in a war against Xerxes and at an age that exceeded the average lifespan of his kin by 50 percent. At that time, Greek men who survived childhood died, on average, between the ages of 30 and 40.

Let's double click on that for a second. If the average male lifespan in Europe is about 80 today, then it's pretty epic to imagine a 120-year-old king way back then marching his tiny, impoverished army into war to defend his country from invasion. Yeah, he was tough—and that mental and physical toughness, together with his leadership from the front and willingness to work hard, is what's behind the word "Spartan" as I employ it in this book.

The story of Leonidas and his 300 Spartans has inspired books, movies, toys, candy, and even a Belgian chocolate shop. It also influenced a brand of obstacle course races that even uses a cheer from the movie *300* as its motivational buildup mantra before a race.

"Spartans! What is your profession?"
"Aroo! Aroo! Aroo!"

Leadership, Management, and Fitness

We'll be talking about leadership, management, and fitness in this book. They are integrated concepts. First of all, leadership and management are different but related. I've done hundreds of seminars where I bring in executives from an organization and ask them about the difference between management and leadership. Most of them think that management is bad and leadership is good. I often get comments like, "Managers just want your blood, sweat, and tears," but leaders "inspire you to be a better version of yourself." I can understand where that perspective comes from.

Most of us serve in organizations under people whose titles are "manager," not "leader," and so we've tied the definition of management to our personal views of those people in those positions. If we have a bad manager, we think managers are bad. And we might be stuck with a bad manager for years, drilling that bad-manager worldview into us over an extended period containing thousands of experiences. However, people in organizations rarely have the title of "leader." A leader is someone we choose to follow. If we have a bad leader, we can just follow someone else, so we don't think of that person as a leader anymore. That means we never spend extended periods of time under bad leaders, at least not knowingly aware that they are bad. So we have long engagements with bad managers and short engagements with bad leaders. I'm pretty sure that's where the leadership-good and management-bad ideas came from.

I define leadership (in part) as the stewardship of unrealized resources and management as the stewardship of existing resources. To me, this is a fundamental difference between the skills of management and leadership: the nature of a stewarded resource. To illustrate the point, I use everyone's favorite case study: Apple.

In 1997, Apple was 90 days away from bankruptcy. The company decided to purchase NeXT for $429 million. The acquisition brought two resources to Apple: the NeXTSTEP operating system and Steve Jobs.

Jobs came to Apple as interim CEO for 90 days to recruit a new CEO and set the company right. He had big ideas, but a visionary leader was not really what the company needed at that moment. Visionary leaders are great when the company has money to burn on R&D and experimentation. They are good with push-product marketing and don't mind incurring losses on their way to disruptive discoveries.

But when a company is struggling to allocate limited resources under pressure, what it really needs is a strong manager. In the case of Apple, the manager's name was Fred Anderson. While Jobs was scratching his head over what to do next and whether or not the company could be saved, Anderson was the guy who restructured the finances behind the scenes, including selling stock to their competitor, Microsoft, for $150 million in investment. This bought enough time for Apple to make a shift in its product offering. What shift?

Jobs's focus was on network machines when he came on as CEO as that was what he was working on at NeXT, but that kind of product was not going to save Apple. The demand was not strong enough in the market for that kind of product to generate enough income within enough time to save the company. Apple needed someone who could steer the company in the direction of a market demand that actually existed, not a future demand that needed to be created.

Again, it was Fred Anderson who pushed Jobs to switch from network machines to a low-end consumer product. That consumer product was the iMac. Once Jobs had management direction, the visionary leadership component could thrive again. The all-in-one, rounded, and colorful case design was received as exactly the kind of product that both fit the market demand and made good use of Apple's existing resources. The iMac turned the company from nearly a billion USD in losses to $300 million in profit in 1998. Profits doubled to $600 million in 1999.

That was the comeback for Apple. Anderson, the quiet, steady, research-driven finance manager in the background, was the company's real hero during the storm. If it weren't for him, Apple may have burned the last of its working capital building network machines that no one wanted. Jobs gets the credit for the visionary breakthroughs that came later. He drove the iPod, iPhone, iPad, and other great disruptive technology.

So the moral of the story? When you have money to burn, steer the power in the direction of your visionary leaders; these are the ones who will take greater risks, invest in R&D, and discover the disruptive innovations. But when times are tough, find and empower your best managers. The managers will generally be quieter and perhaps less popular because they tend to make hard choices like cost cutting or partnering with "the enemy," as in the case of Apple.

Leadership and management go hand in hand, but there are definitely times when one hand should be intentionally stronger than the other. I'll talk about both in this book because we need both. That's why I use the term "chief executive." It's not indicative of a manager or a leader per se—could be either. Whether leader or manager, I'm a Spartan. You will be too.

Mental and Physical Fitness

Fitness is addressed from both a physical and mental perspective. The body is nothing without the mind. I won't go into depth here because it's the subject of chapter 1, but physical and mental fitness are significant contributors to bottom-line success both in personal self-efficacy and in organizations. Fitter organizations make more money. I present this argument in the chapters that follow.

Individual, Interpersonal, Organizational

I talk about management, leadership, and fitness from the individual, interpersonal, and organizational perspectives as well. You'll have tools for use on yourself and those beside you, and if you're leading an organization, you'll know what to do with your people as well.

Science and Experience

I also talk about these things from both a personal and a scientific perspective. I tell stories from my life that fit into these themes and make sure that whatever I claim, I cite so that any management-studies geeks in the crowd can follow my research. I hope that you'll laugh a little at the pillars that got me to where I am now and that you'll really take to mind the research that's presented as a motivator to get you aligned to becoming a stronger version of yourself. Spartans embrace the science.

Is This Book Only for Gerard-Butler Alpha-Male Leaders with Abs?

I don't have (visible) abs. And, yes, the designation "executive" is in the title, but the material will benefit anyone in a leadership or management position in any organization. It is intended for anyone wanting to become a high-performing leader in any capacity: work, home, religion; all of these arenas will benefit from you being at your finest. The fact is that people like to follow strong people, and you have the opportunity every day to become you at your strongest.

I have felt that I'm at my finest when I am challenging myself to do things that I'm only 80 percent sure I can do, like a Spartan race, or a degree, or writing this book. When I take on something that scares me a little bit, it's exciting, and I need to ratchet up my performance in some area or collect a new skill in order to accomplish it. I want the same for you. You won't know what you're capable of unless you are setting goals for yourself that you are a little unsure you can accomplish. You'll learn just as much in the process of trying as you will from the success or failure. So I wouldn't worry too much about the achievement part just yet.

If you want some encouraging and challenging input from an expert coach with 20 years of leadership experience, then this book is for you. You may not like everything I have to say, and that's okay too. Just skip the sections that you feel you're too sensitive to finish. Ha!

Ladies, I know the content might seem a bit masculine. Unfortunately, most historical leaders, like Leonidas, were men.

I am also a man and am writing from my own experience. Plus, at the time of writing, the majority of executives in the world are still men. But this book is for you as well. All of the principles I discuss are gender-neutral unless I'm specific otherwise. I do hope the gender balance in business gets better, both in representation and in pay. As you read this, just note that the principles are human, not male specific, and many women in history have exercised the kind of Spartan leadership that I am promoting here as well.

In Leonidas's case, his wife, Gorgo, was an equally inspiring character. Herodotus names very few women in his ancient *Histories*, but shining among them is Gorgo. She was the daughter, wife, and mother of three kings of Sparta. She spent her entire life in leadership positions and was presumably a pretty tough leader at that.

Ahead of the Persian invasion of Greece, an exile named Demaratus sent a message to Sparta to warn Leonidas of the coming war. The message was sensitive, and so it was engraved on a wooden tablet and covered with wax. No one could determine what was meant by the wax-covered wood—that is, until Gorgo saw it and discovered that once the wax was scraped off, the message could be read. The warning gave the Spartans time to recruit and prepare their defense. For that discovery, she has been credited as being the world's first female cryptanalyst (Kahn, 1996).

The Parallel Lives by the ancient historian Plutarch records an interesting suprapatriarchal exchange in which a foreign woman remarked to Gorgo, "You Spartan women are the only ones who rule their men," to which Gorgo replied, "Yes, we are the only ones that give birth to men" (Plutarch, 1914). Presumably, her stance on women in leadership was egalitarian and two millennia ahead of her time. But this was not just in word. She also ruled both as queen and as a regular contributor to the government of Sparta. She is noted in Herodotus's works as a presence in the court and advisor to the king (Knox, Bowersock, & Burkert, 1979).

So, yes, my brilliant and powerful female colleagues, when I talk of a Spartan, you're included (although probably by midway through the first chapter, you'll hate me for it).

What Kind of Book Is This?

As I said above, it's a bit of mental and physical fitness and a bit of management and leadership. Mostly, it's a book of pillars aimed at helping to encourage you to be at your very best, no matter what your social role is. Each pillar is intended to be read and digested over the course of a week, so six pillars over six weeks. I hope that will make the material a bit more digestible for you.

The first element in each pillar is a workout. That's right: it's time to hit the gym. I'm not kidding, and, yes, you need to do it (or at least try it). The workouts are specifically designed to connect to the pillar for that week and should serve as a physical reminder of the material you've read and help you to connect with the impact of the pillar and remember it better. You only have to do the workout once, and you should always take the advice of your physician or personal trainer before doing these sorts of things. If you're already a bit fit, do the Spartan Workout. If you're less fit, do the MiniSpartan Workout. I've included a scaled-down version so that the majority of readers can do it.

Each pillar then contains a few small subtopics, all aimed at helping you to be at your mental, physical, and organizational best. Again, with a specific workout in place for that week, you'll connect your body with the concepts, and that will help you to remember them. You'll also have a few mental exercises and pillar-specific tasks to complete.

Spartan Core Finisher
At the end of each pillar, I highlight some of the major principles that I've communicated to give you a quick reference guide to that pillar for later review.

Defining Moments
I also give you a few suggested milestones in your personal leadership development. These are things that you can strive for, and you'll see your own progress in attaining some of them.

Questions for Consideration
Finally, I include a few guiding questions for you to ask yourself to see how well you remember the material and have integrated it into your life.

My hope is that all of these added features will make it more interactive for you. Of course, if there's anything you really hate about this book, don't waste your mental energy on hating me; just throw it away, or use it to balance out the patio table on the porch, or start that bonfire you've been meaning to have with the family. If you really want to respond to me, I'm happy to hear from you at www.drcorrieblock.com.

Don't Be Fat; Be Fit

MiniSpartan Workout
Warmup
5-minute walk at 4 kph (2.5 mph) on the treadmill

Workout
Run for a minute; walk for a minute. Run at 8–12 kph (5–7.5 mph) for one minute. Then go back down to 4 kph (2.5 mph) for one minute. Ten rounds for a total of 20 minutes.

Follow this with a 10-minute uphill walk. You can walk up a real hill or set the treadmill to 4 kph (2.5 mph) on an incline of 5–8 degrees.

Cooldown
Walk back down the hill or set the treadmill to 3–4 kph (2–2.5 mph) for 10 minutes on zero incline.

Spartan Workout
Warmup
5-minute jog at 7–9 kph (4–5.5 mph) on the treadmill

Workout
Sprint, as fast as you can, for 30 seconds, with a 1-minute rest between sprints. Zero incline, 10 rounds.

Follow this with a 20-minute brisk walk uphill. Set the treadmill to 6 kph (4 mph) on a challenging incline for the walk.

Cooldown
Walk back down the hill or set the treadmill to 4.5 kph (3 mph) for 10 minutes.

This is a great workout for fat burning and for busy managers. Have you ever looked at the body of an endurance runner? They're thin, lean, light. Now check out the body of a sprinter. Just as lean but packed with muscle. You get my point. Run fast. Do it over and over again. Don't be lazy.

During the one-minute rests between each sprint, remind yourself of your values, your mission in life, your goals for this year, and a couple of the life goals still on your bucket list. This will help to connect your mind and intention with what you are doing physically with your body.

We're talking about fitness this week, and we'll be discussing three kinds of fat in your life: physical fat, mental fat, and organizational fat. These correspond with the biopsychosocial model of mind, body, and environment, if you're into business pop psychology. The mind and body are intrinsically linked. What you do in one arena influences the other. And the body and environment are intrinsically linked. What happens in one affects the other. These will be reoccurring themes throughout the book.

I Am a Spartan!

I have a sweet tooth, which is why I exercise. I used to be a free-style inline skater (ramps and jumps and scraped knees) and did a bit of downhill skiing and mountain biking in my late teens and early twenties in Canada, so I had some base fitness, but that had long disappeared by 2013. I used to be skinny like a rake. If you looked at pictures from my wedding when I was 20 years old, I was a scrawny little thing with long hair. I wore baggy jeans and a plaid jacket to make myself look a bit bigger than my size 28 waist showed. I ate Mars bars, drank Coke Slurpees, and had something from McDonald's nearly every day. I never paid attention to my diet, and exercise was more of a hobby than a discipline, so I just kept on my merry way.

When I was about 25, my metabolism slowed down. My son was born, and I didn't lose any of the baby weight at all (eye roll). I had eaten my way through the pregnancy in solidarity with my first wife but didn't give birth to anything in the end, and so there was no end. My weight hovered around 110 kg (242 lb.) for the next decade or so. By the time I was 37, I was the poster boy for the chubby consultant. My suits were tight, and I didn't like the way I looked or felt.

The breakpoint for me was at the beach sometime in March 2013. My closest friend in the world called me a "fat, ugly, pathetic little man." She apologized later, of course. It was horrible, though, and it broke my heart a bit, but it did influence me to change. The very next day, I signed up to join a gym. My initial commitment was to exercise for one hour every day for 21 days, no days off. I knew how to kick my own ass in education and consulting work, so I figured it couldn't be that much different to kick my ass in the gym. But it was different. Very different.

It was *a lot* easier. I hated the first few days, but the addictive neurochemicals produced in the brain during and after exercise are a real thing, it turns out. I slowly trained my brain to expect hits of dopamine, serotonin, adrenaline, and endorphins from my time working out. After a while, my brain started to accept and anticipate the gym as a source of brain drugs, and after the 21 days, I didn't stop going. I kept it up, going five to six days a week after that. I lost 17 kg (37 lb.) in the first three months, and my first wife, who had let herself go a bit as well, got motivated by my daily grind and decided to get fit herself. She joined a regular bootcamp. She's now one of the fittest people I know.

Michelle was the trainer that the gym assigned to get me started. Three free sessions with Michelle were intended to get me going. She showed me the equipment and offered some structured training for me. We also filled out a couple of forms, on which one of the questions was "Why are you joining the gym at this time?" She continued, "Is there a wedding coming up? Do you want to look good at the beach? Do you want abs? What's your fitness goal?"

"I'm here to earn the right to eat whatever the fuck I want when I'm not here," I responded.

She laughed. "Well, that's honest, I guess. I've never heard that one before."

I was serious, though. My abs were deeply buried under a decade of chocolates and fried yummy things, and I had no intention of changing my eating habits. I love food—bad food. I love sugar and fat and salt, all together if possible. One of my favorite snacks is French fries and a chocolate Frosty from Wendy's. I scoop up the Frosty with the fries and eat them together. The combination of sweet and salty, cold and hot, soft and crispy all at the same time ... it's like a party in my mouth. So satisfying. I wanted to keep eating that and still lose some of the belly that weighed me down. And I did.

It's been a few years since then, and I still don't have abs. But that doesn't matter to me anymore. I'm the kind of guy I would want to hang out with in an apocalypse. In fact, if the world goes to hell in a handbasket, with zombies and all, come find me. I'm smart, I can lift heavy, and I run indefinitely.

After the initial few months at the gym, I got into CrossFit, and for the next few years, I toned up. I hit my personal records in lifting at the age of 41. I weighed 82 kg (180 lb.), and I benched 100 kg (220 lb.) and deadlifted 200 kg (440 lb.). I'm happy with those numbers and see no need to beat them. But I also paid the price for pushing too hard. I have weak tendons in my shoulders, which I discovered after an MRI following my second major shoulder injury, which I'll tell you about later. Anyway, I blew out my shoulders and spent a year in rehab.

I really missed CrossFit, though. I missed the intensity of it and the community that comes from that intensity in a crowd. I wanted to do something really challenging like that again, so a friend of mine recommended obstacle course running.

I'm not a runner. I hate running, in fact. It's boring, and jarring on the knees and ankles, and boring, and repetitive, and dull, and boring.

But running in soft sand, over mountains, on loose rocks, carrying buckets of gravel, climbing walls, and throwing spears ... that didn't sound boring at all.

I remember the first time I ran an obstacle course race. It was in fall 2015, a 5 km (3-mile) Spartan Sprint in Dubai. It was a fitness challenge that I had set for myself, and I'll be real with you folks: I didn't know if I would be able to finish it. I had never run 5 km (3 miles) in my life.

I was in okay shape, but it was still hard. Running a Spartan race in Dubai meant running in soft sand for most of it. That's a special kind of pain for the calves. I wasn't used to it. I cramped up, and it was a slow trudge for a while. But there I was, the first race of my life, carrying a bucket of rocks up a hill, thinking, *This isn't so bad. I can do this.* Until I couldn't.

When you fail an obstacle in a Spartan race, you are required to earn your way through the obstacle by doing 30 burpees. I think I did 120 burpees during my first 5 km (3-mile) race. One of the race marshals told me that since I was running an open race and not a competitive one, I didn't have to do the burpees. But I did them anyway because my goal was to finish the race, not just to get to the finish line. Now it's one of my mantras while running obstacle course races: "Every meter, every burpee." I say it to myself whenever I'm tempted to shortcut an obstacle or skip the burpees.

To a real Spartan runner, there's a big difference between getting to the finish line and finishing the race. But every race starts the same. Some caffeine-fueled fitness guru grabs a bullhorn and yells out, "Spartans! What is your profession?" to which we all respond, "Aroo! Aroo! Aroo!"

Physical Fitness

Does it matter if a leader is physically fit? You bet it does. In a decade-long study of 1,500 executives, Limbach and Sonnenburg (2015) demonstrated that a CEO's physical fitness is associated with higher firm profitability and higher M&A announcement returns, in line with other known benefits of physical fitness such as stress management, cognitive functioning, and overall job performance. The bottom line is fitter leaders make more money, for themselves and their shareholders.

What do we mean by fitness? Well, to the point, we mean fit to run, not fit for golf. The study mentioned above measured firm performance in companies whose CEOs had run a marathon in a given year. They showed that physically fit CEOs "are associated with significantly higher return on assets and more free cash flow"; additionally, "abnormal stock returns to M&A announcements are significantly higher, and are less likely to be negative, when the bidding firm's boss is fit" (Limbach & Sonnenburg, 2015, pp. 4–5).

In contrast, golf-playing CEOs were studied by Biggerstaff, Cicero, and Puckett (2017), who found that the 25 percent of CEOs who played the most rounds of golf each year were associated with significantly poorer-than-average firm performance (i.e., less money). So, no, we're not talking about a walk around the block every night leader or a Saturday morning golf game type of leader; we're talking about leaders who are fit to run. Spartan leaders.

Here's the tough truth: if you're in good physical health, you'll think more clearly, have greater concentration during tough meetings and decision making, have more stamina during a negotiation than your counterpart, and be able to keep up with all the millennials driving you nuts at the office. All of that will lead to better motivation modeling for your team and higher-quality decision making for you. End result: better firm performance (i.e., more money for everyone).

So if you want to improve your net margin this year, how about you start by dropping a couple of inches on your waistline? No, I'm not kidding. You're reading a book called *Spartan CEO*; you knew this was coming. It's fair play.

As a good business leader and good manager, you might want to encourage the same in your staff. One of the managers I know takes her team to run a half marathon twice a year. Another manager friend of mine takes his team to a Spartan or Tough Mudder race every year.

Some businesses are improving the physical fitness of their employees by changing the environment in which they work. They are adding sit/stand desks and exercise balls or backless chairs for seating. Some have fully functional gyms in the building. Many companies have recognized the benefits of having a higher quality of air and light in the workplace. These small changes influence the physical well-being of employees through small adjustments to the environment. These changes result in higher attention spans and better productivity, not to mention improved loyalty to the organization. When people feel cared for, their health improves, and productivity goes up.

For your own personal fitness, I recommend exercising for no less than 45 minutes, at least three times per week. This is the minimum unless you have a medical condition that prevents you from doing so. Actually, now that I think of it, Nick Vujicic is the CEO of a small company, and he swims, surfs, skydives ... and he has no arms and no legs. So, yeah, all of your excuses are lame.

Mental Fitness

The brain is like a muscle. You can make it stronger by exercising it, and when you stop exercising it, guess what happens? Yup, it gets weaker. Are you forgetting things? Names? Places? Details of deals you were supposed to follow up on? Important birthdays perhaps? Do you feel sluggish at certain times of the day? Finding it harder to concentrate for long periods of time?

It gets dangerous when you, as a leader, begin outsourcing your decision-making competence to your staff. If you can't understand or can't be bothered to pay attention to the numbers being reported to you for decision-making purposes, then you need to delegate those decisions immediately. If you are the decision maker, you must be mentally fit enough to manage the volume and quality of information required to make the decisions that you choose not to delegate. Your whole team is counting on you. Poor mental fitness is just a recipe for lazy leadership and financial disaster.

Symptoms of this kind of mental obesity may include:

- Delayed responses to requests for input, like e-mails
- Lack of market knowledge

- Lack of understanding of the firm's products, services, or procedures
- Pride over reaching a high level in Candy Crush or Angry Birds
- Lack of engagement on the details of new business ventures
- Lack of knowledge of new best practices in the industry
- Lack of knowledge of global disruptors such as robotics, blockchain, artificial intelligence, the science of happiness, etc.
- Hanging out only with people from one's own race and/ or religion

If that sounds like it might be you, you're fat. Mentally fat. And it's time to get in shape. Your people are counting on you for leadership, and that includes thought leadership, so you need to be able to think at a level that your people can respect.

After 20 years in consulting, I've met dozens of mentally fat leaders. The problem is they are often aware of it; they just don't know what to do about it. Something happened to them along the way, and they stopped reading books, they stopped educating themselves, they stopped participating in conferences and conventions. They redirected their mental energy to easier things like playing golf, or watching TV, or sitting around in majlises drinking tea. They can hide behind their fancy positions and titles with everyone else, but they can't hide from me. And if an external consultant can walk in and know within a day that the leader is mentally obese and running well behind some of the top staff in the thinking department, then the business is in trouble.

Fight

There are two common ways for leaders to hide their insecurity over their lack of mental fitness, and they are as old as time: fight or flight. Fight leaders will try to mask their incompetence by yelling, intimidating, or berating their team members. Since they lack the mental agility to manage the strategy conversation rationally, they beat their chests like gorillas by asking irrelevant questions loudly, demanding extraneous work, or picking on little things that they still feel competent in, like document formatting. For these leaders, a show of strength is intended to make their mental opponent (a team member who's smarter than them) back down through intimidation. It's immature and unbecoming of a Spartan.

Remember when I said I'd be gender-specific if required? Well, women leaders who are mentally obese tend to manipulate rather than intimidate. Their show of strength to ward off an intelligent team member they perceive as a threat is a lot subtler, in my experience. They will subtly dismiss or ignore their perceived competitor's input. They will be passively aggressive by refusing to respond to e-mails, calls, messages, or questions. They marginalize those they feel threatened by. In extreme cases, I have even heard of women flirting their way out of a competence challenge at work. I'm not saying this is a common practice; what I'm saying is that mentally unfit people of both genders tend to revert to premodern (Neanderthal?) tactics for establishing dominance when they reach the limits of their ability to mentally reason and understand things.

Don't get me wrong: there are definitely times when raising your voice is a good thing. Like when your running mate is slowing down, and you know he or she is tired, but there's still 4 km (2.5 miles) to go. Then, by all means, yell at that person. When a Spartan executive yells (and we *do* yell), it's to motivate and encourage the team. It's to give direction in an economic war to quickly cover an unprotected flank or to respond to a surprise attack from the competition. It's to project inspirational strength, to give assurance to our people that we are strong enough to lead them, and to encourage them also to raise their voices so that we may benefit from their input, encouragement, and energy.

Flight

The second common response of the mentally obese is flight. Those managers who know that they are not competent enough to lead their own staff sometimes manage their incompetence by being absent. They avoid the office, avoid meetings, and avoid communications because, deep down, they see every interaction with their staff as an opportunity for their mental obesity to be exposed and for them to be shamed.

They will show up to work late and leave early. They don't schedule meetings with their people but attempt to hide their avoidance orientation in a "door is always open" policy. Some managers will have an open-door policy and be great, active, mentally engaged leaders as well, seeking out their people and remaining involved in the processes. The mentally obese will simply say, "The door is always open" but then physically close the door and often be absent.

The mentally obese will sometimes avoid discovery by avoiding communications as well. They simply don't respond to e-mails or requests for input because, internally, they are fearful of asking a question or making a comment that exposes their mental obesity. They fear the shame that will come from being discovered as a less competent leader than is required for their position on the team.

Feather
But there's a third, less common, and more socially acceptable form of masking one's mental obesity: visionary misdirection. I see this a lot in macroleaders (the opposite of micromanagers). The term isn't mine; it comes from Henry Mintzberg (2013). A micromanager is someone who does the job of the staff or refuses to delegate decision-making authority to those around who are competent to take it on. In contrast, a macroleader is someone who is so visionary, so far above the fray of the everyday business, that he or she has lost touch with the mechanics of the organization or the needs of the client. They have a 40,000-foot view of the company but aren't relevant on the ground.

These kinds of leaders are prone to compensating for their mental laziness by being inspiring for its own sake. Yes, they are eloquent in speech and motivational to listen to. They may connect well with people and be really friendly, but they don't really have a handle on the fundamentals of the business anymore. They distract their people from their incompetence by being fun and beautiful, like a peacock.

Workout
Okay, so the first step in being fit is to admit that you're not as fit as you'd like to be. The second step in being fit is to choose a behavior that leads you in the direction of an articulated goal. Here are a couple of examples.

Perhaps you want to be more effective as a leader with your team:

GOAL 1: I will read one leadership book every month.
DISCIPLINE 1: I will read for no less than 90 minutes, three days a week.

Or perhaps you want to be more industry competent so that you can be better engaged with your team during strategy discussions:

GOAL 2: I will seek input from 12 outside sources every month.
DISCIPLINE 2: Read one industry-specific blog and listen to two industry-specific podcasts every week.

Or perhaps you just want to build your attention span so that you can be more effective in negotiations:

GOAL 3: I will increase my focused attention span to 30 minutes within 60 days.
DISCIPLINE 3: I will meditate or practice mindfulness for five minutes every day, increasing by five minutes per day every week for six weeks.

You get the idea. Start with a goal and then choose a discipline that will lead you to that goal.

Organizational Fitness

As a business leader, you may have noticed some fat deposits growing in your organization. These are unused resources, perhaps in the form of underutilized capacity, underperforming staff, misappropriated funds, empty spaces, dead stock, and other missed opportunities. All of these things represent resources that could and should be utilized for the benefit of the community but are not, due mostly to poor management, and so the organization carries deposits of untapped energy in these forms of organizational fat.

Typically, consulting companies that are tasked with a restructuring project concentrate on one particular metric for weight loss, layoffs, which only represent one type of fat, underutilized staff. They can often take a very short-term approach to provide customer value by convincing the consulting client that cutting staff reduces expenses and improves efficiency, resulting in weight loss. So they look to cut as many people as they can get away with, without hindering the core operations of the organization. This is intended to reduce the excess capacity in the organization and is even often referred to as "trimming the fat."

A consultant with a single metric for success, cost cutting, is a bit like a surgeon with a single metric for success, weight loss. Imagine going to the doctor to improve your health. You say something like, "Hey, Doc, I don't think my body is performing as well as it should be. Can you tell me what to do?"

"What's your ultimate goal here?"

"Weight loss. I want to be lean."

"Okay, then lean it is. First, we'll do a bit of light liposuction around the tummy and thighs and maybe a bit under the chin. But since we want to lose as much weight as possible, we can also remove half of your stomach, the large intestine, half of your small intestine, the gall bladder, and appendix. There's nothing that your kidneys are doing that can't be outsourced to an Indian dialysis machine, so we can get rid of those too. And since you're a woman, we can take out your uterus. After that's done, you'll have a few pounds of extra skin ... we can make you leaner by getting rid of that as well. Imagine all the weight you'll lose."

"Won't that be difficult?"

Because many business leaders still don't understand what fitness in an organization looks like, they sign on to the abusive surgeon's weight loss program. Job cuts ensue, and the rumor starts in the organization: Who's next? Am I safe? Am I still a valuable part of the body? What do I need to do to survive this round of fat trimming? The community goes through trauma, friends are torn apart, and the workplace becomes an unsafe environment.

Those who leave the organization in rounds of redundancies like this pay the initial price. They are excised from the body. They are forcibly removed from a community to which they have been dedicating 50 percent of their conscious lives, every day, for the past number of years. Their livelihood is cut off, and their families often go into turmoil as they try to transfer into a new body and develop a new blood supply in the form of a new household income.

They tell stories about the asshole bosses in their previous community who so callously and casually removed them from their community. They talk about those they used to work beside as victims of newly expanded job descriptions with fresh and impossible key performance indicators (KPIs). They become antiambassadors of their previous community. They talk badly about the brand, the leadership, and the product or service that they used to represent in the market. Like a jilted lover, they use their inside information to expose weaknesses in the organization, its unique selling proposition, and its operating procedures. They quietly spread whatever rumors will cause the most pain to their previous employer, a community that once fed their family and then at once ejected them to save money and widen the margin. By cutting them out of the community, the bad surgeon has poisoned the market, slowly eroding your brand equity over the course of that person's lifetime.

But surely with the big consulting firms prescribing these kinds of surgeries daily, there can't be anything wrong with them, right? Surely the research will support that it's just a normal business practice, right, Dr. Corrie?

Good question, Reader. Let's have a look.

Burgard, Brand, and House (2007) have found that involuntary job loss is related to significantly poorer health and mental depression, even when the populations are corrected statistically for other causes of poor physical and mental health. This supports earlier research that found depression to be the most frequently reported mental cost of redundancies (Kasl & Jones, 2000). A follow-up study noted that, especially in the case of redundancies among older employees, their spouses may need therapy to deal with the loss as well (Siegel, Bradley, Gallo, & Kasl, 2003). This is a big enough topic that the *Journal of Managerial Psychology* dedicated a whole issue in 2012 to the psychological effects of job loss (Karren, 2012).

A recent US study of job loss during a recession found that there is a statistically significant increase in hazard of death from redundancies (Noelke & Beckfield, 2014). Experiencing a redundancy is associated with increases in heart disease (Gallo, Bradley, & Falba, 2004; Gallo et al., 2006) and risk of suicide (Garcy & Vågerö, 2013). The suicide study was conducted in Sweden, by the way, which ranked as the ninth happiest country in the world according to the UN 2018 World Happiness Report. Even in the best countries on earth, redundancies tend to kill people, statistically speaking.

That's right, forward thinkers and business leaders: if you let enough of your staff go, statistically, some of them will die from it. Chew on that for a minute.

Now listen up. Here's the thing: when you cut organs out of your body, they die, unless they are immediately transplanted into a new body. When you cut people out of the community that has been supplying their family, they die too. They begin the slow march toward depression, anxiety, trust loss, and heart disease, all of which increase their hazard of dying and decrease their quality of life. It's a grossly negligent strategy for cost savings in any company that has people, happiness, employee satisfaction, general health, or sustainability anywhere in its strategy document.

If an outside consultant is prescribing job cuts as a weight-loss solution, he or she is probably just a bad surgeon. There are better ways to get fit.

So here's what you do. First things first. To keep as much of your body intact as you can, you have to let go of the weight-loss goal and start in the direction of a fitness goal. Weight loss and fitness are two very different things, physically and organizationally. You can lose weight by chopping off a leg, but it'll impact your fitness a great deal as well. And that's what many business leaders also don't understand.

Okay, maybe you're totally at peace with letting a hundred employees go, knowing that a few could die as a direct result, but what of those left behind? Do you really expect better productivity from a body that has just undergone major weight-loss surgery? If you underwent the weight-loss surgery prescribed above, how long do you think your personal rehabilitation would take? How long before you could walk again? Years.

If you ask a common millennial MBA consultant what the effects of redundancies are in an organization, he or she is likely to describe them in positive terms: increased net profit, decreased salary expenditure, increased role clarity, decreased process redundancies, etc. He or she will tell you that in the long run, it's not a big deal. But if you ask an experienced business doctor what the effects of redundancies are on the same organization, he or she will tell you quite another story. It's a big deal. It's a big, terrifying, scary deal.

But it's different in companies, Dr. Corrie. Companies aren't bodies, and the surgery metaphor doesn't work in business like that. Companies that go through redundancies continue on past those dark days and sometimes do really well. Those who remain are relieved; they have more responsibility, sure, but they are happy to still have a job, and they tend to perform better, don't they, Doctor?

Great question, Reader. Let's review what we've learned.

By the '90s, we already knew that redundancies in a company resulted in feelings of anger, fear, guilt, and shock among the managers who survived the culling (Brockner, 1990; Kozlowski, Chao, Smith, & Hedlund, 1993). These resulted in the managers who remained in the company being more risk averse and less dedicated to their work (Smith & Vickers, 1994). The managers who survive the cuts carry lower levels of organizational commitment, trust, and motivation for years, often into their next career steps.

Cutting jobs ensures that remaining employees become more loyal to themselves and their own personal visions for their lives over the collective vision of the company (Handy, 1998; Reilly, Brett, & Stroh, 1993). Those who survive become survivalists. Are you shocked? I'm not. There is a hidden contract between the employee and the corporate community. The agreement is that if the employee looks out for the community's best interests, the community will provide for and protect the employee. A round of layoffs teaches the employee that the community is not committed to provide for or protect its people, and so the employees learn to protect themselves. They learn that their work environment is unsafe and cannot be counted on to care for the employees and their families.

The intended effect of redundancies is increased productivity and competitiveness, but researchers disagree with this widely held assumption. Worrall, Campbell, and Cooper (2000, p. 463), for example, have reported, "The main consequence of redundancy on survivors is increased task overload and reduced role clarity as redundancy is far more effective at removing people from an organization than removing the tasks that they used to do with residual, disembodied tasks being cascaded down the hierarchy."

By the way, future thinkers and innovative leaders, we (business doctors) knew all of this 20 years ago! That's right: the consulting industry ignored the research in favor of short-term, bottom-line gains even after we knew that the long-term psychological effects on both the displaced and the survivors of a culling were (deathly?) grave. Why? Because that's how the consulting industry makes its money, and that's how bosses are judged by their boards of directors: on organizational weight loss, not on organizational fitness. It's time for new metrics. It's time to be fit.

Liposuction is a fool's path to fitness. Fat is stored energy. So what if we looked at potential redundancy victims as organizationally stored capacity instead? Can you convert fat to muscle by working hard? Well, in a physical body, no; fat gets burned as muscle is formed. But in an organization, yes, you can convert extra capacity into innovation, agility, and offense. What is 30 seconds of top-speed sprinting in an organization? What does that look like to you?

Personally, I like the balanced scorecard (BSC) (Kaplan & Norton, 1992) approach. Most of you will know what that is already, so I won't dwell here for long. Basically, the BSC approach balances the common, past-focused, singular metric of financial performance with other indicators of future success. If you are also paying attention to your customers' feedback, improving your internal processes, and investing in learning and development, you will have a better indicator of your future results rather than just looking at the past results in a financial statement.

It's a bit like training your way to fitness. If you continue to focus your attention on the unwanted fat, you'll be more inclined to go through liposuction and spend weeks or months in rehabilitation. Instead, you could be spending those same weeks and months doing tried and tested exercises that lead to future success in fitness, things like cardio, moving heavy things around, jumping over stuff. The principles are essentially the same in business: if you eat healthy and exercise, you will become fitter. In an organization, if you pay attention to your customer, improve your processes, and make sure your staff is in a constant learning environment, your organization will naturally progress to the place where you're not organizationally fat but fit.

What does a process improvement sprint look like? Start by getting the team together and telling them that, as a team, you all have five working days to identify and solve a problem or eliminate a minimum of three steps from any process in the department.

After running a few sprints, your team members will be in a challenging and focused environment as they engage in continuous improvement, are dedicated to their clientele, and are learning daily. They will solve problems before they are articulated, innovate products and services immediately upon market feedback, and feel loyal to and engaged in a community that's investing in their personal and career development.

As with any diet/exercise scheme, there are a ton of brands out there to choose from if you don't like the basics of BSC (Caldart &

Ricart, 2004; Neely, Adams, & Kennerley, 2002; Razmi & Ghasemi, 2015; Ruef, 1997; Voelpel, Leibold, & Mahmoud, 2004). My point is choose what we know works (organizational fitness), not what we know doesn't work (organizational liposuction). Spartan leaders know what needs to be done to get fit physically, mentally, and organizationally.

Don't be lazy. And don't be fat.

At the beginning of this pillar, I prescribed sprinting as a way to physically burn fat. Here are a few exercises that will help lead you to organizational fitness:

1. Strategic alignment
2. Process engineering
3. Customer surveys
4. Customer appreciation programs
5. Product/service innovation sessions
6. Executive coaching
7. Key result area (KRA)/KPI design
8. Market research

Yes, every one of these requires an output of energy and resources (as does physical exercise), but so does organizational liposuction. At least these investments will lead to long-term fitness instead of long-term rehab.

Now, even I know that there are times when a market disruption is so massive that companies begin to drown in their stored capacity, and perhaps a bit of liposuction is required to save the life of the organization. So if you find that you have either redundancy papers or insolvency papers to fill out today, then my heart goes with you. If that's the choice you're making, and you've engaged a good business doctor (for the organization) and a good executive coach (for you), then you may consider a few layoffs. However, the way you conduct this surgery is perhaps even more important than the decision to undergo it.

You will need to prepare for the surgery and for the rehabilitation period. Just like in physical surgery, there are preparatory prescriptions and rehabilitation exercises that reduce the impact of the surgery and speed up the healing process. And, yes, there's research on those things too.

If you must cut off a part of the body to save the rest of it, then it's imperative that the proper rehabilitation precautions are in place. There must be a significant investment in procedure and communication to mitigate the inevitable feelings of injustice that remain in the organization after a culling (Madden, 2015). Specifically, it is important that:

- employees receive honest, straightforward, and detailed information;
- employees comprehend why downsizing is unavoidable;
- the antecedents of downsizing are made clear for employees;
- employees are not uncertain about their futures;
- employees find the selection criteria fair and reasonable;
- victims receive fair treatment and are given proper redress;
- increased postredundancy workloads are justly shared;

- employees are involved, to a greater or less extent, in the decision-making processes;
- survivors also receive appropriate treatment, and the organization offers training opportunities and facilitates the acquisition of marketable knowledge;
- the organization ensures employees' autonomy, varied work tasks, and opportunities for development to increase work motivation (Krasz, 2005).

You must honor your commitment to your teams. They are counting on you to provide the kind of leadership that will facilitate the community in being strong enough that it can compete with other communities over economic resources so that all of their families will be cared for and all of their personal goals will be met. Don't betray them by being physically fat, mentally fat, or organizationally fat. They deserve the best from you. They're counting on you. Fit body, fit mind, fit community.

Spartan Core Finisher

1. Your physical health has a statistically significant impact on the bottom-line performance of your team, department, or company. You know what needs to be done. Get it done.
2. Your mental fitness impacts your ability to both manage and lead your team. When you try to hide your obesity through fight, flight, or feathering, they take note, and they will question your competence as a leader behind your back. Don't avoid the work; avoid the shame of not working. Stay in front by being mentally fit.

3. Your organization needs to be fit, not to "lose weight." And even if it could stand to lose a bit of excess, it's better to burn that excess up in capacity building than to liposuction it off with a bad consultant and pay the price in a year of community rehabilitation. Be smart, think long term, and do what is needed to stay healthy as a corporate community. Surgery is a last resort.

Defining Moments

1. Your first 30-second sprint at 23 kph (14.3 mph)
2. Reading a whole leadership book in less than a week
3. Reading 12 books in a year
4. Cutting organizational expenditure by 10 percent without a single redundancy
5. Running your first marathon

Questions for Consideration

1. When was the last time you could bend over and touch your toes?
2. How many hours a week do you spend playing video games, watching TV, or surfing social media?
3. How many hours a week do you spend reading or listening to industry podcasts?
4. What is your mental fitness plan?
5. Do you need a physical fitness coach or an executive coach to get you going?

You Can Do More Than You Know

MiniSpartan Workout
Warmup
400 m jog followed by 2 rounds of:

- 10 air squats
- 10 sit-ups
- 5 pushups (on your knees if you prefer)

Workout
Declining ladder: 18-15-12-9-6-3

In the first set, you will do 18 reps. In the second set, you will do 15 reps, and then 12 in the third, and so on until in the last set, you will do 3 reps of each of these:

- kettlebell swings: 12–16 kg (26.5 – 35 lb.) for guys, 8 kg (18 lb.) for ladies
- Step-ups (24" box or use an exercise step, alternating feet)
- Burpees (if you don't know it, Google it. Haha! You'll *love* these!)

Finisher: After you finish the ladder, you need to complete the following:

- 20 kettlebell deadlifts
- 12 burpees (with a jump, clap your hands above your head each time)

Cooldown

- Walk or light jog for 3 minutes or 400 m
- 10 minutes of stretching

Spartan Workout
Warmup
400 m run followed by 3 rounds of:

- 20 air squats
- 15 sit-ups
- 10 pushups

Workout
Declining ladder: 24-21-18-15-12-9-6-3 for time (i.e., as fast as you can)

In the first set, you will do 24 reps. In the second set, you will do 21 reps, and then 18 in the third, and so on until in the last set, you will do 3 reps of each of these:

- Kettlebell swings (24 kg / 53 lb. for guys, 16 kg / 35 lb. for ladies)
- Box jumps (32" for guys, 24" for ladies)

- Burpees (if you don't know it, Google it. Haha! You'll *love* these!)

Finisher: After you finish the ladder, you need to complete the following:

- 24 goblet squats with the kettlebell
- 24 box-over burpees (a burpee and then you climb over the box)
- 400 m run (as fast as you can)

Cooldown

- Cry for a minute (if required)
- Walk or light jog for 3 minutes or 400 m
- 10 minutes of stretching

This workout is amazing for stretching your understanding of what you can do. Each set requires a little less than the set before, and so you get into a pattern of declining expectations for what your body will be required to do. By the time you reach the set where only three of each exercise is required, most of the glycogen in your muscles will be used up, and you'll probably be in that foggy state where you can't quite think straight.

You'll feel the relief of the set of three burpees, and your mind will give you a small hit of dopamine for accomplishing the ladder and maybe start to produce lactic acid since you are expecting a completion reward. But then there's the finisher. You'll say to yourself, *What do you mean I'm not done? WTF? Right ... the finisher.* And here's the point of the exercise. Can you pick up the kettlebell again, with the timer still running, and work your way through that last set? There are three exercises, so you'll need a bit of brain power to remind yourself of them, and you'll need to find some muscle strength that a moment ago you had allowed yourself to think you wouldn't need.

The purpose of the workout is to get you to the point where you believe you have completed it, and then more is required of you. That will force you to make a choice to move forward in spite of the physiological and neurochemical pressures to stop. It's a matter of will. But, trust me, you can do more than you know.

The First Step of the Last 15 km (9 miles) Is the Hardest

It was 5:00 a.m. My alarm started screaming at me, and I struggled to roll over to turn it off. My back felt like it was made of scales. My everything hurt. I dropped one leg over the side of the bed, and it hit the floor like a stone. I had run a Spartan Beast before, twice, so I knew what the morning after felt like. Sore muscles, joints, and tendons clawing out for ice, or sauna, or both. Blisters breaking into their morning song, demanding attention like a toddler with a full diaper. I slowly got dressed, pulling one sock after the other onto my tired and whingy legs. I didn't want to stand. But there they were, taunting me, scowling at me. My shoes.

I picked them up and braced myself for the ordeal. Pulling the shoes on over my blistered feet and feeling that place where my injured left heel had rubbed raw against the blown-out back of the shoe. I stood up but only for a second and collapsed again with a look on my face that crossed from shock to terror as I counted the cost. There's at least 15 km (9 miles) to go.

Why am I doing this? I thought.

"Just to see if you can," I replied.

"This is stupid. No one is going to disparage me if I stop now. I did the Beast yesterday already."

"Yeah, but all your friends are waiting to hear about you finishing today. You posted it on social media. You'd never live it down with Danish. He knows, and he's cheering for you."

"Screw you, Corrie. Asshole! Fine, I'll go, but if we get injured, it's *your* fault!"

An hour later, I was at the starting line—again. The Spartan Beast was a 23 km (14-mile) race the previous day that resulted in my tired and raw feet. The Spartan Super was starting any minute now. It was another 15 km (9-mile) obstacle course race. The organizer got up onto the stage and started yelling to encourage us, to rev us up. I was not revved.

"Spartans! What is your profession?" he shouted.

"Aroo! Aroo! Aroo!" the crowd replied.

But not me. I was on my knees, desperately trying to shove a small patch of folded-up cardboard into the back of my left shoe to create a makeshift pad between my destroyed shoe and my destroyed heel. I was swearing at myself under my breath, almost certain that even if I started this race, I couldn't possibly finish it.

"Three! Two! One! GO!"

That first step over the starting line, that was the furthest I had ever run in this kind of a race. I was tired, and in pain, and every step I took set a personal record. Every meter was a new frontier, a distance I'd never been to before, and a challenge that I was uncertain I could accomplish because I had never before tried. In front of me lay another 15 km (9-mile) track over loose rock and soft sand, scaling walls, and carrying buckets of gravel. Could I do it? I didn't know. Even then.

So I did what I could do. I ran the next hundred meters. I was pretty sure I could make it another hundred meters. I was nearly positive. Almost fully convinced. All that I lacked was the experience of having done it before. So I did it. One hundred meters at a time.

I finished the race, all 15 km (9 miles), in an average time, some-where in the 60th percentile of those running in my age bracket. If my goal had been to win, I would have run fresh and healed, not blistered and bleeding from the Beast the day before. But my goal was to finish. To see if I could do it. To satisfy my own curi-osity about my upper endurance limits and to test my own will and self-discipline. I collapsed onto the grass after the finish line, exhausted. With only an hour to rest. I wasn't finished.

I had completed the Super, the 15 km (9-mile) race, sure, but my test wasn't over yet. I pulled the soaked mush of cardboard out of the heel of my shoe. I resisted the temptation to remove my shoe completely out of fear that I might not put it on again. I walked around in a futile attempt to keep the lactic acid at bay, and after 45 minutes, I was back at the starting line again. Yup, another 5 km (3-mile) race to run.

I met a guy named Ahmed on the trail. He had placed second in his age group in the Beast the day before. But he was running the Trifecta as well this weekend, and we found comfort in each other's stories of pain and suffering as we encouraged one another through the trails and trials once again. At one point, I turned to him and told him I was exhausted, and with 3 km (2 miles) to go, unsure if I would make it across the finish line.

"You can do more than you think," he said.

I jumped up onto the A-frame and climbed to the top to find a woman trapped there, crying. She lacked the courage to pull herself over the top and down the other side. I climbed over to her and asked her name.

"Miriam." She whimpered a bit and then apologized for her fear and weakness.

"You can do more than you think, Miriam."

I smiled and reached out my hand. I hooked my arm under hers and pulled her over the top of the frame, guarding her descent down the other side. She thanked me as I joined up with Ahmed again, and we continued running.

Just before the finish line, after the rope climb and before the fire jump, there was a wall. It was a little taller than I stood with my hands stretched out above my head. Ahmed and I looked at each other. My best friend was on the side of the track to cheer me on, and she said that as we approached the wall, we both stopped, put our hands on our knees, and let out a big sigh of defeat.

So close: 43 km (27 miles) and only one wall left to go.

"I can do more than I think," I said. And we jumped up and pulled ourselves, slow and groaning, over the wall.

It was both painful and rewarding. I had done something that I was only reasonably confident that I could do. I had done it with open wounds on my feet and the muscle soreness that was already dominating me from yesterday and then that morning. I did it. You can, too, and so can your colleagues.

Confidence Is a Skill, Not a Talent

Earlier this year, I spoke briefly at the annual kickoff event for Al Masaood Automobiles in Abu Dhabi, UAE. I had been working on strategy and leadership development with their top three tiers of management for about six months already. The kickoff event had some very interesting artifacts on display. On popup banners around the room were the words "BETTER, FASTER, and STRONGER."

I was invited to speak about 90 minutes before I got up to do so. I was conducting their leadership development program in the same hotel, so I was on hand for the event. I walked on stage without any preparation at all, and I told a couple of great stories about meaningful management and personal strategies in business, but in the back of my head, what I was really thinking about was those words I was seeing throughout the room.

Better.
Presumably, this is a call to be better than before. Better than I was yesterday. Better than *we* were yesterday, last month, last year perhaps. I definitely think we should be measuring ourselves against our own past performance, but there is something a little unnerving and a bit sinister in the word that I hadn't noticed before. For me to be "better," I would have to accomplish something that I had not accomplished before. My existing bank of experiences was invalid, deficient, for "better."

Faster.
There it was again … faster than I was? Faster than I've ever been, perhaps. For that to happen, I would have to run at a speed I've never run at before. I would have to achieve a new top pace for what I was doing—sales, marketing, accounting, cleaning, hiring. Whatever I was doing in my corporate community, I would have to do it faster than ever. I had no frame of reference for what that kind of speed felt like because, by definition, I had never experienced it before. All my experience was instantly inadequate.

Stronger.
Stronger happens when we endure a challenge or ordeal that we've never endured before. In the physical sense, our muscles get stronger when, through strain of use, they break. The healing

is what makes them stronger. Again, none of my previous experience would suffice if I was to be at my strongest ever. My history was inadequate in this better, faster, stronger future that we were all being called to join in on.

It was invigorating, energizing, empowering, encouraging, and fun to be in the room with a couple of hundred seriously focused and passionate people, all cheering and chanting and finding their connection with each other and their shared vision as a team. But all of those years of experience, all of their collective education, their communal wisdom—all of the strategies for performance they had all collected along the way were casually dismissed as yesterday's success in light of what we were being called to achieve in tomorrow's experiences: better, faster, and stronger.

By the way, public speaking is tough. I've heard that public speaking is the most common phobia among humans. I still get anxious when I get up to speak. So when I ran up to the stage with nothing to say and no time to prepare, it wasn't because I was unafraid; it was because I was confident. Some people would be absolutely crippled by the task of having to stand up at a large event, face the crowd, and instantly say something meaningful.

So why do some people succeed and others fail if they seem from the outside to be fairly equal in terms of education and experience? How can one person stand up at an event and give an impromptu and meaningful speech, while another declines behind the most common human fear? How can one manager do such an incredible job with turning a company around and an equally competent one fail at the same challenge? How can one footballer make the critical game-winning goal in the last minute and another miss it? Why are some people able to pull themselves up after a termination, divorce, or death in the family, and others simply allow their lives to drift away from them in an ongoing wave of despair? The research of Hollenbeck and Hall (2004) asked precisely these questions. For that reason, I'm going to draw considerably from their research for this conversation.

Before we begin, self-confidence should not be confused with self-esteem or self-worth. Confidence is your assessment of your abilities in relation to the requirements of a specific task. Self-esteem or self-worth are your assessments of your personal value as a member of the human community: how much you like yourself. But you need a lot more than self-esteem to do things; you need actual skills, abilities, competencies, and knowledge (Bandura, 1997). Believing you are worthy and valued is an excellent, positive frame of mind, but it won't get you through a 43 km (27-mile) Spartan Trifecta. Confidence is a matter of actual capability. It doesn't matter how much self-esteem Nick Vujicic has; he'll never win an Olympic medal in the pole vault. (Sorry, Nick. Love ya, man!)

Self-confidence is, by definition, the judgment that you are able to do something. That confidence is not based on what your actual abilities are or even what the actual challenge is going to require but your perception of those things. It's also not a general state of mind but context dependent. Confidence is related to a particular activity or task, not to everything. So you can be confident in one thing and not in another. No one is self-confident all the time (Hollenbeck & Hall, 2004). Confidence is not the same as optimism, hope, or resilience but has been studied as a corollary with those qualities under the heading of psychological capital (Luthans, 2002; Luthans, Avolio, Avey, & Norman, 2007) and as a core component of leadership (Popper & Mayseless, 2007).

Perhaps you've come across a personality test that indicates you as a self-confident person. I don't think this can be accurate, strictly speaking, nor do I want it to be accurate. If someone is truly self-confident as a dominant personality trait, then they, by definition, perceive themselves to already possess the ability to do absolutely everything they could possibly be required to do. This only happens from a psychological perspective if:

- CATEGORY 1: The self-confident person is omnitalented, possesses godlike intelligence and Olympic strength, and is potentially immortal; or,
- CATEGORY 2: The self-confident person is limiting their chosen experiences to those in which they already have experience or knowledge; or (and perhaps most likely),
- CATEGORY 3: The self-confident person's perception of their ability to do absolutely everything is a delusion, not a character trait.

John Maxwell said that when confidence exceeds competence, it's called arrogance. It's an accurate description but also a pretty common quality among humans. What one person calls arrogance, another calls "positive thinking" or "positive self-image." If a positive view of oneself is inaccurate, which is the higher value? Should we have a self-deceiving positive view or a less positive but more accurate view of ourselves and our abilities?

Well, as it turns out, a bit of self-deception may be a good thing. Bénabou and Tirole (2002) have suggested that people tend to have inaccurately positive views of themselves for a few reasons.

- Thinking good of oneself is less painful than thinking more badly (more accurately) of oneself.
- Believing in your abilities, even if you don't have them, makes it easier to get other people to believe you have those abilities as well.
- Believing you have more abilities than you have makes it more likely that you will take on greater challenges and stick to them when things get tough.

So there seems to be a utilitarian purpose for arrogance from a psychological perspective. We tend to have a rosier-than-accurate view of our participation in unpleasant past events, such as a termination or a breakup, as well as a rosier-than-statistically-probable view of our future. Besides, people who expect to fail, more often do. More confident people who fail are more likely to leverage the failure as a learning experience, developing personal resilience (Luthans, Vogelgesang, & Lester, 2006). We don't want to err on the side of thinking of ourselves as losers, and we don't want to be devastated by failures by running low on confidence, so a touch of unfounded optimism is probably a good thing.

In another twist of psychology, I've found that some people who describe themselves as self-confident are not arrogant at all but lazy. They fit into category 2 above. They simply limit their attempted tasks to those things in which they already have experience. They don't try anything new, better, faster, or stronger, thereby avoiding the risk of failure, thereby always, in their own minds, succeeding. That's not self-confidence; that's cowardice. The easiest path to success is to attempt nothing of consequence as a matter of choice.

Also, I don't want it to be true that confidence is a personality trait. Think about it: if you think that self-confidence is a personality trait, then you're also likely to believe that you are either born with it or born without it. If that's true, then what hope do we have of bettering ourselves? On the contrary, confidence can be built and broken. "Thus, for our purposes of developing leaders and leadership qualities, people with self-confidence are made, not born. The bottom line, then, is that self-confidence is one of the self-management factors that people can influence, such as fitness and education" (Hollenbeck & Hall, 2004, p. 259).

Building Self-Confidence

I am a pretty confident person, I think. But it's not a character trait like introversion or intelligence; it's a context-conditional state of mind, developed over time. I am often in contexts where I have to attempt something that I've never attempted before. Sometimes I fail miserably, but more often I succeed. The reward either way is that I collect the experience of having attempted something that I was unsure I could do, and being successful more often than not builds up a pattern in my mind that says that I'm more likely than not to be able to achieve a challenge that I attempt in the future.

The good news, then, is that you can train your brain to be more confident by attempting and achieving tasks that you have a reasonable chance of succeeding in. It's that caveat there, "reasonable chance," that most people struggle with. So start with small increments. Two percent faster, 2 percent stronger, 2 percent better. Taking a 2 percent jump in something will give you a reasonable chance of success. Then when you succeed, you'll feel amazing about it, and you'll build up confidence to take on the next 2, 5, and 15 percent. You can change your view of yourself by building up a pattern of small wins.

People with a more accurate view of their own capabilities tend to achieve a higher ratio of wins when they attempt challenges that bear the risk of failure. This leads to an increasing level of comfort in taking calculated risks, which is the feeling of confidence. Research is strong that people with a higher level of confidence:

1. are better at problem solving
2. set and achieve higher goals than less confident people
3. choose their colleagues, projects, and challenges differently than less confident people (Hollenbeck & Hall, 2004)

In other words, people who build up a pattern of confidence tend to take on the 15 percent increase attempts rather than the 2 percent increase attempts, and they succeed more often because they have learned in the process of increasing trial and error to make better use of both their current capabilities and those of the people they surround themselves with.

Hollenbeck and Hall (2004) have listed four inputs that contribute to a person's sense of confidence, which I have adapted slightly and arranged into internal and external inputs of emotion and experience.

	Emotion	Experience
Internal	How I feel about doing it	Things I've already done
External	How others feel about doing it, or me doing it	Things I've seen other people do

Internal Experience

This is perhaps the most powerful input. I'm more likely to attempt things that I've never done if I have experience doing similar things in the past. The Trifecta races that I described at the beginning of this chapter are a good example. I had run races like those before. I had completed more than 20 obstacle course races, and I knew roughly what to expect. Even though the challenge was longer and would test my endurance, the strength and competencies required to run and complete the obstacles were already banked in my memory.

When I started my company, Paragon Consulting, it was a new challenge, for sure, but I had started six other companies in the past. It was a new territory but not entirely foreign. Being in consultancy can be nerve-racking. I was telling my best friend about how I live never knowing if I'll have any income in a month or two, to which she replied, "You're crazy."

"Well, I'm used to it."

My previous experience with winning and losing bids, executing projects, taking on new projects, and proposing successful solutions all led me to believe that starting a new company, though costly and unstable, was ground I could (probably) cover (more likely than not). Certainty is a luxury of the arrogant. The truth is I didn't know until I tried, but my previous experiences led me to believe that I had the stuff required to make it happen.

It was the same again when I sat down to write this book, by the way. I've written books before, but this was the first one of this kind. So I knew I had the capabilities, but it was (is) still challenging.

When you are looking to build confidence, you'll want to start by stretching yourself in an arena in which you already have competency and capability. Start with lower risk-of-failure attempts. Take on some small wins to build momentum, and then you can hit the accelerator and take on some higher risk-of-failure leaps once you build your confidence up.

Others' Experience
The experience of others is also a big piece of input in confidence building. I knew that others had run the Trifecta in two days before, and I could gauge my physical and mental capabilities as commensurate to theirs. I had friends who had run marathons,

Ironman races, and other major endurance challenges. I knew that they were more experienced than I was, but they weren't in much better physical shape than I was.

In the business world, it's called modeling or inspiration. We see in others the kind of success that we would like to have. And if we judge ourselves to be commensurately competent and capable as those we are looking at, we are more likely to have the confidence to attempt that kind of success. I know leaders with similar competencies and capabilities to my own who have started consultancies and been successful. I gathered confidence from looking at other people who had done what I was going to attempt as a challenge.

So if you're looking to build confidence, make sure you're filling your mind with the stories of people who have done something similar, with similar resources to those that you have. I find business biographies really helpful for this. You can also use other peoples' failures as input to build your confidence, especially if you can identify that a weakness that led to their failure is something that you have as a strength. If you have education or experience that compensates for the mistake that your model made that led to a failure in a particular task, then that's quality data for you to build confidence with.

Internal Emotion

Your emotional reaction to a challenge may be the most powerful limiter in the confidence-building process. How do I feel about what I'm facing? Does it energize me or frighten me? Or both? Our ability to isolate and control our emotions is a major factor in confidence. As I said, it was still scary for me to stand up and speak at the kickoff event for Al Masaood. I had experience in speaking meaningfully, and I had seen others with similar skill-sets to mine manage in similar situations. Ultimately, I had to control my emotions and choose a behavior that led me past the fear and through the new challenge.

Our physical and mental state at the time of a challenge is a big piece of input in confidence building. If you're tired, or hungry, or just coming out of a defeat of some kind, you naturally won't feel as confident about the challenge you're facing now. Keep in mind that the way you feel doesn't have any bearing on your actual abilities, only on your perception of them. So feeling defeated doesn't mean you don't have what it takes to conquer the new opportunity; it just means that it'll be harder for you to assess your capabilities as adequate to the task. It's a perception problem.

Mark Twain said, "Courage is resistance to fear, mastery of fear—not absence of fear. Except a creature be part coward it is not a compliment to say it is brave; it is merely a loose mis-application of the word." Franklin D. Roosevelt told it this way: "Courage is not the absence of fear, but rather the assessment that something else is more important than fear." I personally prefer the meme that developed online as a result of them both: "Courage is not the absence of fear but the mastery of it."

When I started Paragon Consulting, just as when I stepped onto the stage to speak, I was afraid. I recognized it, measured it, owned it, and deemed it an unworthy internal opponent to my confidence that I would be able to achieve my aim.

Here's an interesting brain hack for you: The human brain uses the same chemicals to express anxiety and excitement. The hypothalamus triggers the brain to dilate the pupils, start sweating, increase your heart rate, and increase your breathing rate, both when you're afraid and when you're excited. That's why haunted houses are a thing. And roller coasters. I love a good roller coaster.

The difference between being on a roller coaster and being in a vehicle actually spinning out of control isn't the fear but the anticipation of fear. It's the nucleus accumbens, a small piece of your brain's limbic system, that gives you a chemical reward for anticipating the fearful situation before it happens (Klucken et al., 2009). So when the fearful thing actually happens, you experience it as excitement. It's evolution's way of teaching our brains to expect the unexpected. So when you're faced with something that you feel afraid of and you're pretty sure you should be afraid, one of the easy brain hacks is to tell yourself how excited you are.

If you ever get to see the video of my speech to the Al Masaood Group, you'll notice that the first thing I say when I grab the microphone is, "I'm *so excited* to be here!" That was an intentional choice. That was me hijacking my fear into excitement by awakening the nucleus accumbens. Try it sometime. It's pretty cool.

External Emotion
This is often called persuasion. It's the other people's voices in your head that tell you that you can do something. It's the encouragement of a trusted teacher, a loving parent, and a supportive manager who tells you that they believe in you. It's also the tool of every talented salesperson who convinces a prospective client that they are capable of affording a luxury item, whether they are actually capable or not.

On the second day of the Trifecta races, with blistered and bleeding feet and no internal motivation left, I could hear the voices of my kids, friends, even my clients telling me that they believed in me, that I could do it. I wasn't so sure at the time. Standing at the starting line with another 15 km (9-mile) trail waiting for me, I wasn't sure I believed in myself. Their voices added to my confidence.

When I expressed my concerns about starting Paragon, my mentors and close friends invariably told me that they were "absolutely certain" that I would do very well in the endeavor. I wasn't as certain as they were, but their voices gave me confidence anyway. I trusted them. They were the kinds of people who knew me well, and they were the kinds of people who had done similar things in the past. Some of them had a clearer view of me than I did, and others had personal experience having succeeded in what I was about to attempt. Both of those added to my confidence.

So if you're looking to build your own confidence, talk to people who have experience with you and with people who have experience with the challenge you're facing. How others felt about attempting the challenge you're facing and how others feel about you attempting the same challenge will both be informative pieces of input in your path to rational self-confidence.

Building Confidence in Others

People aren't born with self-confidence. Even the most self-confident people can be broken. Self-confidence comes from success, experience, and the organization's environment. The leader's most important role is to instil confidence in people. They must dare to take risks and responsibility. You must back them up if they make mistakes. (Carlzon, 1989)

Being the voice of encouragement that helps to build confidence in others is not very difficult at all. Salespeople do it all the time: "That looks great on you!" "You're worth it!" "It's not a matter of whether or not you can afford it but whether you can afford not to." "Today's missed opportunity is tomorrow's regret." "I own one myself; you'll love it."

Sales is an amazing arena in which specialist confidence builders help us to overcome any remaining lack of confidence that stands between us and the purchase of a new product, service, or experience. We're faced with the external inputs all the time, and we can become those inputs to help people achieve much more than they thought they could.

My son was 17 years old in the fall of 2018. He had run four races with me before, all 5 km (3 miles) long. He enjoyed them, but he's not a passionate athlete. He doesn't play sports or train in the gym or anything like that. He's passionate about video games and filmmaking. So when I asked him to run a 13 km (8-mile) Spartan Super race with me, he was understandably a bit on the fence about the idea.

Think about it from his perspective: the race I asked him to join me in was more than 2.5 times longer than any he had ever run in his whole life. He had the internal experience of having run 5 km (3-mile) races, so he had some idea of what to expect, but to run two and a half of them in succession? That was a whole new ballgame.

Understandably, he was anxious. He even expressed his desire to back out of the race a couple of times (internal emotion). But here's the thing: I had already collected the experience of running the 13 km (8-mile) race a few times. Plus, I was one of the people on the planet who knew him the best. So with my experience and my understanding of his capabilities, I was able to make a pretty calculated assessment of whether or not he would be able to finish it. I just kept telling him that he would be able to do it, in hopes that he would believe me instead of himself and make the attempt.

He trusted my external experience and my external emotion concerning his capabilities, but he still had to feel capable within himself and more excited than afraid when it was time to start the race. He finished it, by the way. It was hard, and he injured his knee pretty badly after the first 2 km (1.25 miles), but he carried on, and we completed the race together. I have a glorious photo of him jumping over the fire at the end, elated at having discovered firsthand what I suspected all along: he was capable of much more than he knew. That built his confidence.

The only way confidence is built in any human being is when they take on a challenge with a reasonable chance of failure and they succeed. They are far more likely to take on the challenge if they are encouraged by someone with more experience than they have and a bit of knowledge of their capabilities. So how do we behave as the kinds of managers/leaders who build confidence in others?

Encourage Them

The first and the best thing you can do is tell people that they can do something that they've never done before. Of course, it helps if you understand their capabilities and competencies enough to make a reasonable assessment of the likelihood of their success. We don't want to set people up for failure; that doesn't build confidence. Any human's actual achievement is directly tied not only to their actual abilities but also to their perception of their abilities, which grow as they attempt new things and gain new abilities. Humans can do only what they first believe they can do, and, often, they need to be convinced.

James is a good friend of mine who owns a small AI consulting firm. He was giving a presentation recently and asked for my feedback at the end. I had to tell him that he lacked confidence in the presentation and that one way of building confidence would be to tell success stories.

"But I don't have any success stories yet. We're just getting started in AI."

"Then tell someone else's stories of how AI turned their company around and helped them to adapt to or cause a disruptive shift," I said. "You can speak with confidence because you have the competency, even though you haven't collected the experience yet. You're the expert in the room."

After that, his presentations got a lot better, and he started getting work in AI. Now he has both the competency and the experience to deliver real-world AI solutions for businesses. All I did was encourage him to tell stories of others who succeeded, and that small change helped James to build the confidence that led to his own success.

Lower the Risk

The risk of failure tends to be correlated with the cost of failure in terms of confidence. People will take on greater risk if the cost of failure is lower. Inversely, if the cost of failure is high, people tend not to want to take the risk unless it is very low. So two ways we as leaders can build the confidence of others is to lower the perceived risk or lower the perceived cost.

We can lower the perceived risk by improving their chances of success. We can do this by improving their quality of information and resources. In a management sense, we can offer to help coach them through a new kind of assignment, or add more tools to their toolbox, or create a transitionary experience, all of which stack the deck in their favor a little more.

For my son, I did this by taking him to a gym three times before the race to do a 10 km (6-mile) run on a treadmill. It was shorter than the 13 km (8-mile) race and much less difficult terrain than the Spartan would be, plus there were no obstacles. However, it was twice as long as the 5 km (3-mile) races that he had run in the past, and this gave him the experience of covering a longer distance on easier terrain. It was a transitionary experience that added to his internal-experience bank and therefore lowered his risk of failure assessment for the 13 km (8-mile) race. He believed a little bit more that he could do it.

Lower the Cost

As leaders, we can mitigate the cost of failure and thereby increase someone else's tolerance for risk. When our teammates are less afraid to fail, then they will be braver to try. Their courage will help them to have better access to their internal-experience and internal-emotional tools, making them more likely to succeed.

Manny was a senior manager in one of my client organizations. During a leadership training program, when we were discussing empowerment, he remarked, "Sometimes it's right to let them know that if they miss a target, they'll be fired, right? I mean you can't have people who don't want to do better."

"No, Manny," I replied. "Absolutely not okay. It is never acceptable in management to threaten someone's livelihood as a motivational tool. Think about it: you've told him that if he makes a mistake, not only will you not defend him, but he will lose his ability to educate his children, feed his family, and care for his parents. Maybe he'll lose his home. What kind of person would make such a threat? That's a horrible cost. Do you think he will work harder? Try new things? Push the boundaries of his capabilities? No way. He's terrified now."

We had a long talk about reducing the risk of failure to make trying something new seem less threatening and less risky. I told him the story of Kyle.

Kyle was an amazing auto mechanic. He was so good that he got promoted to shop manager and had eight other mechanics working under him in the company. The problem was that Kyle didn't make the transition from mechanic to manager very well. He was promoted because he was the best, but that meant that once he became manager, he was working with a staff of eight mechanics who continued to make mistakes that Kyle wouldn't have made.

Kyle decided that the best way to motivate his team was to penalize them for mistakes that weren't caught before the final inspection, but he offered to help them if they needed it in order to avoid problems. Before long, every mechanic on the team was asking Kyle for help with nearly every step, and often they would ask him to do the harder jobs for them. Since Kyle was the best of the mechanics, and he knew that he could do the job better than they could, he often agreed and completed the more complex tasks.

It wasn't long before Kyle was spending all his time repairing vehicles, with a member of his team standing back and watching him. Kyle had unwittingly moved into micromanagement. He was doing the job for his mechanics, and they were avoiding accountability for mistakes. There was no cost for failure because there was no failure at all, because there was no risk at all, because Kyle was doing all the hard stuff. Meanwhile, Kyle was failing as a manager, and his general manager was wondering how such a talented mechanic could be running such an inefficient shop floor.

After a bit of coaching, Kyle decided two things: to take the risk with his staff and to lower the cost of failure. He eliminated the penalty and refused to touch any of the shop tools. If desired, his staff members could ask him to coach them through a tough job, but he would not do it for them. If a repair failed the final inspection, Kyle would take responsibility rather than blame or penalize his mechanics.

His staff had to try things that they'd never done before. If a mistake was made, Kyle stood between the GM and the shop staff, never divulging which mechanic had made the mistake and taking ownership of the error himself. The mechanics started to trust Kyle again, and they gradually grew in confidence, both in their abilities and in Kyle's leadership.

Kyle had lowered the cost of failure, and that encouraged his staff to take on greater risk. They still made mistakes sometimes, but they grew in competence and confidence until one day the GM remarked that it was great to finally see that he had nine Kyles in the shop instead of just the one.

Lower the cost of failure for your team and watch them attempt greater things. If you are frustrated because you think of your staff as incompetent and weak, chances are pretty good that you're leading them to remain that way. Humans can and want to grow, and they will only do that if there is a low enough risk of failure or low enough cost of failure to make the attempt worthwhile.

By the way, there's a residual benefit to you. As you continue to take risks by empowering others around you, and they grow in their confidence, you will grow in yours, specifically leadership confidence. A group of 627 undergrad students were studied to find that leadership confidence was the highest contributor to self-efficacy in career decision making (Paulsen & Betz, 2004). More than confidence in any particular arena of skill, such as math, science, writing, or technology, confidence in leadership was associated with more confident career decision making in general, regardless of gender and cultural differences.

Individuals' belief that they have the skills necessary to complete a career-related task is directly related to their leadership confidence more than their confidence in any particular skill. So if you develop others in their confidence, you'll develop in your leadership confidence, and therefore you'll make better career choices for yourself. How's that for residual benefit? Thank you, science!

A Confident Organization

People are much happier at their jobs when they feel that their work is both challenging and psychologically engaging (Luthans, 2002; Seligman, 2002). For staff members in an organization to want to take on the challenging and engaging work, though, they will need to be in a community that encourages confidence. The Hollenbeck and Hall (2004) study identified seven ways for organizations to build confidence among their employees.

Look for Growers

People in transition or who are looking for a change are good candidates. Don't be distracted by people chasing a job title or waste your efforts trying to build people who are happy where they are. Identify those with a hunger for greater responsibilities or different kinds of competencies. That's where your future leaders are.

Interviews with Leaders

Have teams interview confident leaders within the organization. Alternatively, invite someone from outside to speak to them and share success stories. I did this for Petrofac last year. I joined an auditorium of the managers from the head office in a two-hour discussion on strategy and self-management. People often learn confidence vicariously through the experiences of others.

Encourage Self-Reflection

Get your people to take notes on their development. This can be done during performance appraisals but should be encouraged on an ongoing basis. Ask them to name those around them they would like to emulate and why. Then encourage them to write a few steps for how they can collect the same competencies and experiences that they admire in others.

Explore Personal Purpose

Every person in an organization has a unique view of his or her purpose in life. Helping people be clear about their life goals, vision, and purpose helps them to see whether or not they are moving in the right direction. Sometimes people realize that they are not moving at all. Clarified focus and direction encourage self-development.

Biographies

Have your team members study the life of a leader in their industry or sector. A finance team can learn a lot from studying Warren Buffet together. A design team might read a book about Steve Jobs. An IT team might be encouraged by reading the biography of Jeff Bezos. Having teams study exceptional leaders together gives them something aspirational to talk about and helps them to see where they, too, can be exceptional.

Learning Styles

Have people describe their best and worst learning experiences. From these, it may be possible to distill personal best practices for learning. Some people learn better visually, some are more auditory, and some kinesthetic. Most people benefit from a blend of the three. Some learn better in the morning and some later in the day. Maybe learning has played a role in past failures, and the optimization or correction of learning tactics can, therefore, play a role in future successes.

Coaching

Peer coaching and team coaching can be powerful tools in an organization. Colleagues can coach each other, or process wins and losses in groups with a coach, to work through the individual and team dynamics that lead to improved success. Coaching helps staff members discover their own contributors to success and optimize them. I've read several books on coaching as a leadership skill, but the best and most practical of those was John Whitmore's *Coaching for Performance* (2009), which is now in its fifth edition. I've read it twice.

To this list, we might add team confidence blending. Chowdhury et al. (2002) have studied teams of business students and found that the confidence levels of less confident team members increased when they were teamed up with more confident team members. More confident team members were also less likely to view failure as a negative, even when paired up with less confident team members. In both cases, teams with some members who had higher levels of confidence were more likely to perform well.

Spartan Core Finisher

1. Confidence without competence is arrogance. Competence without confidence is cowardice. Don't get caught in either of those traps. You won't gain in confidence until you've collected a new experience, but know yourself well

enough to find the balance between cowardice and arrogance in terms of taking on new challenges.

2. Be a voice of encouragement and a model of success for others, but don't do their jobs for them. One of the most difficult things for leaders to learn is how to allow their people to fail and then to defend them and encourage them through those tough times.

3. Build a confident organization. A community that learns together grows together. Shared language, open communication, and a learning environment are keys to building the kind of organization that is communally aware of strengths and weaknesses and of which challenges it can take on as a team.

Defining Moments

1. Complete the workout at the beginning of this chapter.
2. Convince someone else that they can accomplish something that they are unsure of but that you think they can achieve.
3. Defend your staff and own their mistakes as your own.
4. Deliver a public speech on anything. Start by telling the audience how excited you are to be there.

Questions for Consideration

1. Where are you crossing the line into arrogance in your life? Be honest with yourself: are you claiming to have competencies and skills that you actually don't have? Don't be a coward; go collect them!

2. Who is watching you, following your life, and learning from you as a model? Is there a way you can be more proactive in building yourself into someone worthy of being emulated?

3. Who needs your encouragement right now? Are there members of your team, or your family, or among your friends who can do more than they think they can? In what ways can you be that external-emotional voice to add confidence to their view of themselves?

4. What skills or abilities do you want that you don't yet have? What's holding you back from collecting them?

5. Who are you looking to as a model for you to follow? Who is doing the thing you would like to be doing? What abilities and experiences do they have that you don't yet have?

Motivation Is Bullshit

MiniSpartan Workout
Warmup
10 air squats and 5 burpees (3 rounds)

Workout
100 wallballs for time: 6 kg (13 lb.) for men, 4 kg (9 lb.) for women

Cooldown
10–15-minute brisk walk

Spartan Workout
Warmup
10 air squats and 5 burpees (5 rounds)

Workout
250 wallballs for time: 9 kg (20 lb.) for men, 6 kg (13 lb.) for women)

Cooldown
Stand straight, touch your toes, and then reach for the sky (10 times)
    Stretching for 10 minutes

This workout will teach you the value of discipline. If you're in good shape, then you'll get to about a hundred before you've had enough. If you're not in good shape, you'll be using my name as a swear word by about 30 or 40 reps. But you need to finish. Scale down the weight of the ball if you want to, but don't skip any of the reps.

Wallballs Require Discipline

When I first started in CrossFit, I went to a small garage-style CrossFit box in Kelowna, British Columbia. I don't remember the name of the trainer, the box, the street, nothing. I was there on vacation and wanted to try CrossFit in an environment where I knew I'd be gone in a few weeks anyway, and if I embarrassed myself, no one knew me.

The very first day, my very first CrossFit WOD (Workout of the Day)—you guessed it: 250 wallballs for time. I'd never done a wallball before, so I had to learn the movement first. Then the timer started, and there were about eight of us, all throwing medicine balls up a wall and catching them, and then dropping down into a squat before repeating the movement. I made it to 15 before I was winded. I wasn't in great shape at that time. I dropped the ball. Literally.

Then I picked it up again. I broke it down into sets of 10, with a small gasping and wheezing session between each set. After 30, my motivation was gone. All the energy that I mustered up to tie my trainers on, drive to the gym, pay the money, carve out time in my day—all that motivation was gone. I was done. I was over it. I wanted to stop.

You'll know your motivation is over when you start arguing yourself out of doing what you motivated yourself to start doing. I went through every argument I could think of.

Who the hell can even do 250 wallballs anyway? That's crazy talk. I'm a business consultant, not an athlete. Throwing medicine balls isn't an area of strength for me. I don't need to be good at this. No one here knows me. I should just go. I can tell I'm the slowest. They're all pushing 80, and I'm still at 37 reps. This is embarrassing. Fuck this. CrossFit is stupid. This is stupid—a stupid cult for stupid people.

By my fiftieth rep, the trainer came over to ask if I was doing okay and let me know that I could get a lighter ball if I wanted but that I had to finish the reps. It was then that I noticed one of the really fit guys, six feet, shirtless, abs that looked like cobblestone, ran outside to puke. Seriously. And no one stopped. We all just kept throwing the balls against the wall. The guy came back in, laughing it off, grabbed his ball, and kept going.

There was something oddly inspiring about that. First of all, it humanized the demigod. He had a weakness, a quiet and banal sort of limit imposed on him by his uncooperative stomach. But did he stop? Nope. He took a sip of water, picked up the medicine ball, and kept on throwing. I had a thought: *I want to be like that.* I don't want to make decisions based on how I feel, and I definitely don't want little things to determine my limits. That's when I dropped the ball again and said it out loud: "One hundred and thirty reps."

"Yeah, dude!" replied the Viking.

I was more than halfway, and Super Fit was watching me. I had a new set of thoughts: *This is hard. It's hard for everyone. Even dude guy over there with his washboard abs and truck-squat legs. It's hard. Two hundred and fifty wallballs is a lot, but I can probably do it. All I need to do right now is the next set of ten.*

I picked up the ball again, now greasy with sweat and difficult to hold. My legs were fighting against me. I was tired and thirsty, and I didn't need to impress anyone in that room. I was down to sets of five at a time, with a good 10 to 20 seconds between sets.

English speakers have developed great swear words to exaggerate most of the carnal pieces of our human experience. Sex, anger, and defecation have all been the inspirations behind our best obscenities, some of which I was yelling already as I crept past the 200-mark. I swore at the ball, the wall, my legs, the trainer, myself—and that's when I noticed I was the only one left. I was still throwing the ball up, and the others had all finished. I was 50 reps behind the next slowest person in the room. But perhaps I could be the most disciplined, I thought.

The trainer stood behind me. "Pick up the ball, rookie."

"Fuck!"

"Just four more sets. Finish this ten."

"I hate you!"

"Hate is breakfast food. Pick up the ball."

At about 230 reps, I was down to sets of one. That's right: I would pick up the ball, throw it up over the line, and let it fall to the ground. I despised the ball and showed it by allowing it to crash to the ground on its own. No more help from me. Stupid ball.

But I was determined to finish. Not motivated. Determined. I wanted to be able to say that I had done it. I wanted to show the Viking that an overweight consultant, given enough time, could do what he could do. I wanted to prove to myself that I was stronger than I thought I was. And I wanted to see what discipline could really produce.

Two hundred forty-seven.

Two hundred forty-eight.

The other seven people were all standing around me now. I was in a pool of sweat that smelled faintly of Doritos and beer, and they were cheering for me.

"C'mon, rookie, you've got this!"

Two hundred forty-nine.

Clapping now. Cheering. A couple of whistles went up and cleared the fog in my head just enough for me to hear them all yelling at the same time:

"Two hundred fifty!"

I collapsed onto the floor and felt my back instantly stick to it. The trainer brought me my water bottle and offered me a fist bump. Then the others took turns standing over me, giving me fist bumps.

I lay there for 10 minutes, gasping, burning, trying not to cry. But I was proud of myself. I had done it. I didn't know the challenge that I would face when I woke up that morning, driven by curiosity and a beer belly to find out what all the CrossFit fuss was about. I was motivated; I wanted to do it, until I hit about 30 reps. After that, motivation was out the window.

So how did I do the following 220 wallballs? Discipline. That's all. When times are hard, it's the only thing that matters.

Motivation Is a Weak Force

Imagine you're sitting in front of your computer and you have a sudden thought that you should get started on that quarterly report that's due at the end of next week. Do you know where that thought comes from?

It's an addict's craving for dopamine. Every human on the planet is addicted to it. It's a good thing; don't worry. Dopamine is sometimes known as the achievement drug. It is produced by and consumed in the brain when you achieve something, like ticking something off of a to-do list, eating fatty or sugary food, having sex, getting a message on WhatsApp, or seeing a cool post on Instagram. On the street, its chemical knockoff is called heroin, so you can understand now how addictive and powerful this drug is. It's the one that keeps us moving in the direction of doing things. From an evolutionary perspective, humans who are motivated to do, to accomplish, to achieve, to move forward have a better chance at surviving. Those who respond to the dopamine craving accomplish more, eat more, have sex more, take more achievement-oriented risks, and are, therefore, more likely to survive and reproduce into the next generation.

But the initial motivation is fleeting. I heard in a TED Talk once that it lasts about 40 seconds, but I'm not sure who said it, so I can't cite it. Mel Robbins famously defends the assertion that you have only five seconds before initial motivation begins to die (Robbins, 2017). In any case, the initiative to change states from doing what you are currently doing to doing something productive that will feed the dopamine craving is short-lived and easily hijacked by two major brain processes.

The first is the amygdala. The amygdala is the kernel of the brain responsible for the fight-or-flight response. It helps you to assess the risks associated with starting on the report (for example) and explores the worry and fear that you might fail in writing it. You might make mistakes and lose the support of people around you. You might lose your reputation or your income. That's a major threat to your security as a human who needs to eat and perhaps feed a family. So the amygdala is the part of the brain that tells you that it may be better for you to simply avoid that particular task in favor of seeking dopamine from an easier source, like a Big Mac.

The second is the brain's wonderful ability to shortcut. Your brain has a registry of all of the sources of dopamine that you have explored in the past. It knows that you can get the dopamine hit you are looking for from a much easier source than writing that report. The report takes a long time, and, sure, the dopamine hit will be larger, but there are a lot of smaller sources that are immediate and require a lot less energy. You could check your Facebook, for example, or get a snack, or go and talk to someone and say something funny so they smile at you. You get dopamine from all of those things. "So why," the shortcutting brain asks, "would you choose to write the long-term, high-effort report over pursuing those short-term, low-effort distractions?" Most humans, most of the time, pursue the low-effort, short-term gains over the long-term ones. The amygdala and the shortcutting function succeed a good deal of the time, so instead of writing the report, you're suddenly reading the entire Wiktionary page on the etymology of "tickle" because you think it's a funny-sounding word.

Even if you do open up the report and start writing, you're doomed to a barrage of distractions looking to hijack your focus toward those easy-shot dopamine fixes. A recent study has shown that the average attention span of someone working in front of a screen (like I am now) is about 40 seconds (Mark, Iqbal, Czerwinski, Johns, & Sano, 2016). So not only do you have only between five and 40 seconds to respond to the impulse for a dopamine fix by doing something productive, but even if you do decide to kick your own ass and write that report, you have 40 seconds before the next distraction tries to take your attention away from it. And there's another one coming 40 seconds after that.

Another amazing study revealed that if you do give in to the distraction torrent and keep feeding your dopamine addiction by scouring YouTube for the top five videos on Beanie Babies, it will take you an average of 23 minutes to regain your focus and get back to your original task (Mark, Gudith, & Klocke, 2008). So your motivation to continue doing what you need to do and your motivation to get back to it once you've been derailed by the dopamine train are both incredibly weak.

The way I see it is Spartan leaders get things done not by tapping into motivation but by recognizing its weaknesses and moving beyond them. The science is telling us that initial motivation lasts for about five seconds and will be challenged every 40 seconds. That's a pretty weak force to have self-help books and human resources programs written on. We need something much more robust.

So what's stronger than motivation? If motivation is a weak force that knocks on the door of our achievement process but then runs away like a coward to knock on other doors, what's the strong force that actually gets us into the "doing" part of "getting it done"?

And if you can get a dopamine hit from achieving something and another dopamine hit from procrastinating, then how does the brain determine which is a higher order of drug hit? How do people choose between one kind of dope hit and another?

Trading Motivation for Discipline
"At some point, the pain of not doing it becomes greater than the pain of doing it" (Stephen Pressfield, *The War of Art*).

A breakthrough study at Vanderbilt University has revealed that some of the differences between whether people are achievement oriented or procrastination oriented aren't in how much they consume dopamine but where (Treadway et al., 2012). Using brain scans, a team of scientists found that those people who choose to work on the report instead of checking Facebook (for example) tend to produce dopamine in the striatum and ventro-medial prefrontal cortex areas of the brain, the parts related to reward and achievement.

Those who choose to leave the report for another day and instead go on wild journeys into the digital history of Avril Lavigne and Chad Kroeger tend to produce dopamine in the anterior insula, a part of the brain associated with risk perception and emotions. So imagine this: those who achieve do so because they get a dope hit from acting on the impulse to act, and those who don't achieve do so because they get a dope hit because they literally "don't feel like it" (i.e., it's too risky).

Q: Why aren't you studying if you know the test is coming up?
A: I don't feel like it.
Q: Why don't you get off the couch and hit the gym?
A: I don't feel like it.
Q: Why don't you quit your dead-end job and chase your dream?
A: I don't feel like it.

You get the point. The fact is you are literally, chemically, addicted to not feeling like it, and it's a heroin-level addiction. The "not feeling like it" is a pretty good indication that you're chasing the right drug but using the wrong part of your brain. You're using the risk-emotion center instead of the reward-achievement center. You're getting your dopamine hit from avoiding risk instead of accomplishing something proactive. Both risk avoidance and proactivity are paths to dopamine. Both serve an evolutionary purpose. But only one of them will lead to the accomplishment of your dreams for your life. The other will help you to avoid the possibility of failure by reducing your output of effort and conserving energy.

It's funny; as an executive coach, I often ask my clients, "Okay, if everything goes according to plan, what will you be doing ten years from now?" Most of them have perfect clarity on this concept. They describe themselves in different jobs, driving different cars, living in different parts of the world. No one says that they'll be exactly where they are and doing what they're doing. There's always some sort of evolution in their story that takes them beyond where they currently are.

But then I ask them a second question: "For things to go according to plan, what will you be doing tomorrow?" This is a really tough one. I get everything from puzzled bewilderment and blank stares to laughing out loud. Why is it so easy for us to choose a clear and defined destination and yet so hard for us to take just one step in its direction?

Activation Energy

Activation energy is the amount of energy required to cause a reaction. In the case of motivation, it's the amount of energy required to turn a fleeting sense of motivation into an actual action or behavior. It's easier to convince yourself to do things in smaller chunks because it takes less effort and lowers the risk of failure. This satisfies both the shortcutting mechanism and the amygdala by lowering the barrier of entry from a lot of effort required to only a little effort required.

I remember when I first decided to pay attention to my physical fitness a few years ago. I told you the story in the introduction to this book. I won't recap it here, but I will tell you right now that one of the secrets to getting it done was to break up the task into smaller tasks. I went from not having gone to the gym in years to going every day for 21 days, no days off. How? By not focusing on the gym.

I told myself a little story instead. I told myself that I really didn't have to go to the gym after all. No one was going to make me do it. Plus, I could be proud of myself for my good intentions if I took a small step, something easier. So I convinced myself that I didn't have to work out, but I did have to pack my gym bag with the right shoes and gear. Then I got a hit of dopamine for doing it. Next, I told myself that I really didn't need to work out, but I did need to put my bag in the car. Another dopamine hit. Then I didn't need to work out, but I really did have to drive to the gym.

The gym was attached to a mall, so I lured myself with the possible escape of going for a coffee or to see a movie. By the time I got to the mall, I had told myself that I didn't need to work out, but I could get a dopamine hit just by checking into the gym with my bag in my hands. You get the idea. Get changed into my workout clothes. Sign into an RPM or circuit class. Gather the equipment. Do one set. Do another set. Until I built up the mental momentum required to get past the weakness of my own motivation. Yes, I seriously had that conversation with myself for at least 10 days, every day. Eventually, some of those steps became patterned behaviors, and I just started to do them without choosing my way into them. They became a habit, one tiny decision at a time. Working out was still hard, but getting my gym bag into the car became normal.

Starting a smaller habit requires lower amounts of activation energy (the mental stuff required to get going). Large changes or larger habits require more activation energy. So the key is to break up that report you need to write (or this very book you're holding) into paragraphs, sentences, or specific inputs you can achieve. Go after one. It's easy. Low effort required. Then once you get that one, set up another one and go after it. That's how we slowly move the production of dopamine from the emotional-risk section of the brain to the reward-achievement section of the brain.

Step one is to honor Mel Robbins's five-second rule. It's a real thing. Hesitation is an opportunity for you to slip into either fear mode or autopilot. Your brain protects you from exerting unnecessary energy by stopping you from doing the activity that requires change or introduces new experiences that may hold a risk of failure. So when something you need to do pops up in your conscious thoughts, and you identify it as something that you should be doing, say it out loud: "Five!"

Robbins suggests counting back from five to hijack your prefrontal cortex during the motivation half-life period of 40 seconds. Counting back from five brings your concentration to the moment of action and distracts you from slipping back into the default mode of risk-avoidance and comfort-seeking biases. Count backward from five to one, and then get off of your mental couch. Getting going will give you a little dopamine hit in the reward center of your brain, which you'll notice because you'll feel a bit proud of yourself just for moving in the right direction. That's your brain telling you (with drugs), "Good job!"

DJ, Turn Up the Bias!

Locus is the science geeks' term for where something originates. For our purposes here, you really only need to know two main concepts: internal versus external locus of control (Rotter, 1966). The locus of control in human cognition governs your worldview about how much control you have over your experience of the world. Someone with an external locus of control will commonly attribute their successes and failures to luck, fate, karma, or divine intervention.

For example, if you see yourself as constantly having to adapt and react to what the world around you is doing, and you often feel like a secondary character in a play or perhaps even a victim of your circumstances, then you probably have an external locus of control. People with an external locus of control see the world as happening *to* them, and they need to be ready to roll with the punches, adapt, and react. They often talk about themselves as being lucky in the face of a success or unlucky in the face of a failure.

I am an internal locus of control person, naturally speaking. My core value is curiosity, and it has governed a good deal of my life. I study, work, train, attempt, and collect competencies because, ultimately, I am an insatiably curious person. An internal locus of control is associated with stronger learning, work performance, happiness, development, and creativity. It's also associated with a person's increased sense of uniqueness, self-awareness, and attention mastery (Domenico & Ryan, 2017). It's the driving force behind my sense of adventure that took me to Estonia and, later, to Yemen and led to my completion of four postgraduate degrees in my spare time. It's a good predictor of performance overall.

But I was raised in a culture with a dominant external locus of control. I was raised in a very religious home, so I was taught to credit God with my successes and blame the devil for my failures. I sometimes still slip into this mode of thinking, especially when I'm under stress or I take a big hit personally. Thinking this way has led to times of really terrible anxiety in my life because I've occasionally seen myself as unable to control my own circumstances.

For example, a number of years ago, I had a business partner in a company that I started in Dubai. He was honorable and well known in the country and was by all accounts considered a man of integrity and strong in his religion. I was really excited to work with him because of his good public reputation and the fact that we got along well as friends. After about 18 months, our fledgling company was hired by another company, in which he was also a partner, to do a couple of acquisition valuations and some corporate architecture for the holdings company that was planning to purchase them. During the discovery process, I learned that my partner and a couple of other employees at the holdings company had been misappropriating funds (a lot of them). I was in a moral dilemma. I had a fiduciary duty to report my findings to the board of directors in the holdings company, but I knew that if I did so, my partner would be discovered. If that happened, my startup company, in which I had invested my life savings with him, would certainly collapse, and I would lose everything I had invested.

I was sick to my stomach. I didn't sleep. I ate too much of the wrong foods, looking for dopamine in the combinations of sugar, salt, and fat. It felt as though the universe was punishing me for something. I lost hope, and I felt powerless in my circumstances. It was that sense of powerlessness and frustration that really tipped me off to my external locus of control. I believed at that time that my experience of the world was something that was happening to me rather than something that I had control over. If you often feel anxious about life and perhaps catch yourself sarcastically saying, "Huh, what could possibly happen next?" then maybe your natural tendency is to think of your life in terms of fate and karma.

Managers with an external locus of control say things like "The market is tough" and "We'll have to see what the higher-ups say about that." They blame the weather, the market, the competition, the customer, other departments, their leadership, and other people for their failures. When something good happens, they say, "Well, that was lucky, right?" or "The competition dropped the ball," or "We caught a good break." They attribute their successes also to the market, the competition, the customer, other departments, and other people, often missing recognition of their own efforts.

On the other side, people who naturally feel that their experience of the world is something they have control over have an internal locus of control. People with an internal locus of control see themselves as the directors of their lives. They choose their experience of the world around them, and they are quicker to attribute their successes and failures to their own efforts.

When things go badly, managers with an internal locus of control will say things like "We didn't try hard enough," or "What did we do wrong?" or "We can learn to improve." When facing a new challenge, they'll say things like "It's up to us; we decide whether this succeeds or fails." When things go well, they tend to recognize success as a direct result of their efforts and those of their teams. They say things like "Good job, team," and "I'm proud of myself and my department for pulling this off."

People who have an internal locus of control tend to be more proactive and, therefore, more productive. They expect to succeed when they put in the effort, so they tend to try harder and, therefore, achieve more. That's not to say that there is a moral attribution toward internal locus of control over external locus of control. They are not good or bad biases in a moral sense, but the science does suggest that if you have an internal locus of control, you'll probably do better in life because you'll attribute your most likely future to your current efforts, and you'll take responsibility for changing your circumstances much more quickly.

There's no statistical correlation between an internal or external locus of control and job satisfaction, by the way (Benischek, 1996). Both types of managers can be very happy at work. Ultimately, the locus of control, like it is in the choosing of behaviors, is really about responsibility. Who is responsible when something good or bad happens in your life? Is it you or some outside force? Did you get the job because you were qualified or because you were at the right place at the right time? Did you lose your investment in a startup because you trusted the wrong partner or because the world is out to get you?

And if you have an external locus of control, can you change it? Will you be more effective in life if you do?

The answer to both of those questions is yes.

So there I was, staring at a mountain of debt that I had accrued to invest in my startup with my honorable friend, and I had a set of balance sheets and expense statements for a totally separate company from which he and a couple of others had been siphoning funds. My childhood bias toward an external locus of control had me pinned against the wall, looking for reasoning in God, luck, and karma, asking, "Why is this happening to me?"

But it wasn't happening *to* me, *per se*. It was just simply happening. I had slipped into an external locus of control bias and allowed myself to sing the "woe is me" song about the potential consequences of what was happening. It took a couple of days of self-pity, but I eventually did catch myself, and knowing a bit about locus of control, I took control. It was a terrible thought process: *Okay, my partner is responsible for his decisions, not fate, not God, and not karma. That's what happened. He made some choices, and I found out about them. Now that I know, I am responsible. I can ignore it, let it go as out of my purview, and finish the job without saying anything if I want to. Of course, that would be an integrity issue that only I would know about, and could I live with that? Probably not. So the other option is to report the anomalies to the board of directors, allow the shit to hit the fan, and potentially lose the company I am currently building.*

Not a great choice, but it was *my* choice, and in making that recognition, I was able to shift from an external to an internal locus of control.

I did report the findings to the board. My partner was understandably emotional about the ordeal. He threatened me and my family, and I stepped down from my own company, having gained a sizable debt for my share of the investment. A number of people took him to court, and last I heard, he was fairly busy dodging a series of arrest warrants.

I left with my integrity, a significant debt, and all of the competencies needed to start another business—and that's exactly what I did. I founded Paragon Consulting after that. It wasn't easy at all. I was depressed for a few months and dragged my feet. Betrayal is a difficult experience for any human to undergo, and even though the subsequent couple of years were really tough financially, I'm proud of myself for taking control of my experience and taking responsibility for my actions. I had trusted poorly, and I had escaped well. I did that. In the process, I also shifted my locus of control back to its natural state.

Some people naturally attribute their experience of the world to their own efforts. Others don't. It's a skill we may have to learn. So how do we learn it?

First, focus on what you can control. You can't control the weather, the market, your competition, or other people. But that doesn't mean that you should blame them for your experience of your life. You have the ability to sift through the barrage of inputs and information to identify what of your experience you can control. Your attitude is the low-hanging fruit. Ask yourself how you would like to face this challenge, task, or goal: pessimistically or optimistically?

No matter how dire the situation, your attitude about how you face it is in your control. Make a choice for optimism. Then start to identify the potential decisions you can make and behaviors/actions you can choose that will lead you toward a positive outcome. You might not be able to choose to have your circumstance suddenly come to an end, but you can choose to face it intentionally and with a good attitude.

Second, inventory your options. What can you do? What choices can you make? In how many different ways can you make them? You'll be surprised how empowering it can be to make an inventory of the most diverse possibilities that you have in your decision-making portfolio. Also, it's a good idea to get an outside opinion at this stage. A friend, a coach, or an advisor is likely to see options on the table that you didn't initially recognize. Those suggestions, no matter how crazy they may seem, increase the breadth of possibilities in front of you, and that gives you more power to choose the one that you want.

Third, make the call. Don't allow the world around you to decide what's next for you. Make a choice and move in the direction of executing that choice as soon as you can. Break down the goal into small steps that require low activation energy. Taking small steps in the direction of an informed and empowered choice will help you to develop a new source of dopamine from those small wins, and you'll gain confidence by knowing that you are navigating a challenge you've never faced before.

Use empowering language to describe your choices, even if you think they suck. Instead of saying, "I don't have any options," you can say, "I don't like my options, but I choose to ..." Instead of saying, "I don't have a choice," you can say, "I choose not to ..." That's much more empowering.

Last, take responsibility, both for the decisions that you made that might have contributed to your current challenge and for the outcome of the decisions that you are making now to address it. Own the possibility of both negative and positive consequences arising from the choices you are making now. You don't have to accurately predict what the outcome of those choices will be, but you can enjoy the feeling of ownership and empowerment no matter what.

That's how I did it. You can too.

If you ask people around me whether I have an internal or external locus of control today, they'll probably tell you that my words betray an external locus, but my behaviors definitely reflect an internal locus. I talk about divine purpose as both an internal and external force, and I talk about karma, God, and fate having a hand in my life. However, when something happens to me, I'm pretty intentional now about choosing my reaction to it.

Discipline in Others

Carrots and sticks have been the dominant tools in employee motivation theory for a very long time, but if you treat people like donkeys, don't be surprised when they start acting like donkeys.

The rewards and punishments methods of the previous century were developed to produce better performance. If you exceed the target, you get promoted or get a bonus. If you miss the target, you get fired. That's the standard deal, in a myriad of variations. But here's the thing, Spartan leaders: if you keep using external motivators, at the very best you will continue to teach your staff to be externally motivated. It may lead to some better performance some of the time, but that's not what you want in the long run. NOT. AT. ALL. There are much more profitable ways of building the kinds of behaviors that lead to corporate success.

Extrinsic Motivation

Carrots are definitely more effective than sticks since their effect on long-term performance is greater and their effect on turnover of expertise is lower (Van der Stede, Wu, & Wu, 2016). But both external carrots and sticks only have some effect under two strong conditions. First, the reward and punishment should be very high stakes. The punishment has to hurt, and the reward has to really delight in order for the employee to perform better. In a study on low-stakes versus high-stakes rewards and punishments, participants made terrible errors in judgment with low-stakes reward systems that they avoided with high-stakes reward systems (Cole, Kanz, & Klapper, 2012). So rule number one: if you offer a bonus, it has to be big enough to matter to them (not to you).

Second, Vroom's expectancy theory agrees with the idea that people are more motivated to do something if there's a reward involved for achievement but adds that they are less likely to perform better if they don't really want the offered reward or if they don't truly believe that they will get the reward in exchange for the achievement (Vroom, 1964). So rule number two: there can be zero doubt that the reward offered will be granted. If there is a lack of trust in the reward being granted, it will not work as a motivator.

Recognition programs are a double-edged sword as well due to the social politics of being human. We naturally compare ourselves to others around us. So when someone who does the same job as we do gets a greater salary or a bigger bonus, we feel it's unjust. We also tend to get demotivated when an all-star favorite is highlighted in spite of our concerted efforts to be recognized, like an employee of the month who's obviously also the teacher's pet, so to speak. Perceptions of social justice and equality can lead to individual recognition having a detrimental effect on the team.

In fact, one study showed that our desire to be recognized above our peers is great enough to outweigh financial rewards for sales performance (Larkin & Pierce, 2012). But this has to be balanced with the effect that such recognition can have on the rest of the team. The same researchers later found that when individual all-stars were highlighted with recognition, high performers who were not highlighted were demotivated enough to result in a 6–8 percent decline in performance (Gubler, Larkin, & Pierce, 2016). This led to an overall performance decline in the team. So recognition is truly a double-edged sword.

You don't have to give up the reward and punishment scheme with your team; just be aware of its limitations and strive for two much more effective leadership tools: intrinsic motivation and discipline. This is where your leadership skills will significantly develop.

Building Internal Locus of Control in Others
Use language of personal responsibility when discussing both successes and failures. Remember, most humans will tend to credit themselves for their successes and blame external forces for their failures. As a team leader, your tendency will be the same. You'll blame the market for a drop in sales, but then as soon as they pick up again, you'll take the credit on account of all your hard work. Your team members will do it too.

Just think about the difference between these two statements:

"I know the market is tough and the target is high, but if you reach it, just think of the bonus you'll receive."

"I know the market is tough and the target is high, so remember your career goal to start your own company in a few years from now, and think of how much smarter, faster, and more effective this challenge will make you."

The first one is externally motivated, and the second is internally motivated. Both are facing the same market difficulties and have the same promise of a bonus if they are successful.

You can encourage personal responsibility for mistakes or failures by reassuring your staff that there's no punishment coming for the problem but that you applaud teammates who take responsibility for their contributions to any failures and learn from them. There are no omnitalented people out there—we're all humans—so embrace the imperfection of the humanity of your team and help them to feel safe in identifying mistakes and taking ownership of them.

Most people get caught in the tide of taking credit and giving away blame. So in case you don't hear it from anyone else, a part of your job, as a leader, is to give away the credit for the things that go right and take the blame when things go wrong. If you can learn to do this, you will reverse the tide among your team. You will be modeling an internal locus of control and helping to build that sense of personal responsibility in your teammates. Over time, they will feel safer in their mistakes, be more honest, take more initiative, and act more responsibly.

Another way you can build an internal locus of control in your team is to be empowering. We all know that they won't do it as well as you can, whatever it is, but their 80 percent quality is much more efficient than your 100 percent. Your feedback and their sense of security with you will develop them into 100 percent quality delivery over time, but your micromanagement will certainly keep them at an 80 percent quality level. There's nothing more frustrating than working with a boss who's not empowering.

Last, connect your team's work with their personal reasons for working. Everyone has personal goals behind their drive for work. They have financial goals, achievement goals, and career development goals that will only be achieved if they truly connect what they are doing with you to those personal reasons for doing it.

Your team members are with you for a reason. They are there because they fundamentally believe that being with you is their fastest, most effective route to achieve their personal life goals. If there was a better way, they would be doing that instead. Tap into that personal motivation for being in their current position, and you'll help develop an internal locus of control in them.

If you aim for nothing, you are certain to achieve it. So help your teammates to be clear on their aims, and watch what happens when they are working for themselves instead of working for you.

Building Discipline in Others
Once a target, KPI, or goal is set and defined, most managers walk away and leave their teammates to their own devices in terms of figuring out how to achieve it. I'm sure you've heard it just as I have from a bad boss: "I don't care how you do it; just get it done." Or maybe you're the bad boss who has said that a few times in your career. Either way, you know how unhelpful that language is.

Remember that your teammates have the same dopamine mechanisms in their brains as you have in yours. Breaking down a KPI into repeatable success-oriented behaviors can lower the activation energy required for them to build those behaviors into patterns in their minds. They need to develop clarity on the behaviors that lead to success and then a clear pattern of choosing those behaviors over time in order to build good habits. Those habits are what will keep them performing when things get difficult.

The bottom line is that extrinsic employee motivation is mostly a waste of time. I have done my share of reading on intrinsic and extrinsic motivation, employee engagement initiatives, and employee happiness, and none of it will matter when things are tough—not for your team and not for you. All that will matter are the cognitive and behavioral disciplines you've cultivated and how well aligned your team members' own personal goals are to their corporate behavior.

The sweetest carrot and sharpest stick are both powerless in the face of intrinsic motivation and self-discipline.

Dreams are plentiful and cheap; every human has them, often passively. Goals are rarer still, for they require clarity and intention. But disciplines—those are very, very expensive. When you find them in others, praise them, and when you develop one of your own, celebrate with pride, for you have unearthed one of the rarest of all the outputs of human hope.

Organizational Discipline

Executives are besieged with challenges, and success in those challenges is in some part due to the confidence of a reasonable chance of success in the face of them, the motivation to get going, and the discipline to keep at the task and see it through. The biggest mistake I see organizations making is hesitation in the face of an opportunity.

Ready.

Fire.

Aim.

That's perhaps the biggest fear of business leaders these days— that they'll pull the trigger on a new product or service just a bit too early and miss the mark(et). And the mark(et) seems to be shifting around so rapidly that it's nearly impossible to tell if you have the correct aim before you've fired. So the cautious voices in business are the ones that warn us not to fire first because we can't reaim. Those cautious voices reflect the default bias of most humans: a bias toward thinking.

In the thinking bias, we believe that if we just have enough information and we analyze it enough, we will be able to make perfect decisions all the time. This is a trap that a lot of organizations fall into. In truth, the amount of information available on the planet is doubling nearly twice a day now. R. B. Fuller was the first to notice that the volume of information was accumulating at an exponential rate (Fuller, 1981). It was roughly doubling every century until World War I, then every 25 years or so until the '80s, then by the time we reached the twenty-first century, it was doubling about every year. Now it's doubling faster than once a day and is continuing to accelerate (Sandle, 2018).

So if the information available on the planet doubles every time you wake up from a nap, what hope do you have of gathering enough of it to make a confident call on an action before you take it? As you can see, the bias toward thinking has hit a critical capacity limit. We need to shift out of that comfort zone and into the realm of design thinking.

Ready.

Accelerate.

Steer.

In design thinking, the bias toward action helps entrepreneurs and business leaders to take steerable actions. It's the basic choice to do something over nothing when you have the option. It's a core leadership principle at Amazon. They define it like this: "Bias for Action: Speed matters in business. Many decisions and actions are reversible and do not need extensive study. We value calculated risk taking" (Amazon, 2019). I like that Amazon has identified this as a leadership quality; it acknowledges the iterative design and the acceptance of risk as individual character traits.

It's that calculated risk taking that really informs this bias and its effectiveness. Remember when we discussed the brain's aversion to risk and how sometimes our brains reward our apathy and risk-avoidance behavior with a hit of dopamine? That's why sometimes this is a tough bias to develop. Thinking will allow your brain time to expose all of the flight rationale behind risk-avoidance behavior (laziness and procrastination). But you can't think your way to a better life, no matter what the self-help books say. Only what you do will matter. And doing something that hasn't been done before requires the acceptance of some measure of risk. It's the same for organizations as it is for individuals.

There are a couple of pitfalls to look out for in the organizational application of a collective bias toward action. For example, doing something can feel better than doing nothing, even if doing something is less likely to lead to success. One study found this to be true among football goalies during penalty kicks. A goalie in the center of the net will stop the ball 33.3 percent of the time. Yet goalies only stay in the center 6.3 percent of the time. Why do they leap when it's clearly not to their statistical advantage? Because with all of that pressure—the crowd cheering, the coach watching, the owner readying his or her pen to extend their con-tract—it feels better to do something instead of nothing (Bar-Eli, Azar, Ritov, Keidar-Levin, & Schein, 2007).

Harvard Business Review (HBR) suggests that this is true of high-performing business leaders as well. There can be an over-developed bias toward action, which leads them to take action all the time, even when it's unnecessary, which leads to fatigue (Gino & Staats, 2015). Business leaders can get burned out by the business of always being action oriented, which can reduce their decision-making quality and increase the chances of errors based on the missing of basic data.

The same HBR article exposed another potential weakness of the bias toward action as the lack of reflection. If we're always run-ning at breakneck speeds, when will we have time to do the itera-tive design fundamentals of feedback and listening? We need to reflect on the causes of our successes and failures and to honor and correct them in empowering and accountable environments. Of course, we don't want to dwell too much on the past, but if we never reflect at all, we won't learn from it either.

So here are some organizational tips to make sure your design thinking process doesn't get out of hand and lead to action-orientation fatigue:

1. Reflect but don't dwell. Take a bit of time to steward the knowledge of success or failure. Reward or correct if required, and then move ahead. We all check the rear-view mirror when we're driving; it's a matter of safety. But we don't stare at it because that, too, is a matter of safety.

2. Require your executives to take vacations. I can't tell you how many times executives have bragged to me—yes, bragged—about how long it's been since their last vacation. Huge red flag! We are humans, not machine parts. Without proper rest, we will never have the mental time to reset, reflect, and rejuvenate ourselves.

3. Mindfulness is a thing. There's a reason a good deal of the Fortune 500 have institutionalized mindfulness. We need to intentionally slow down, or we risk not slowing down at all. Make sure there are mindfulness training initiatives, and opportunities for prayer, meditation, and mindfulness in your workspace. I'll spend more time on this in Pillar 5.

Spartan Core Finisher

1. Mel Robbins's five-second rule is a pretty good tool for developing a bias toward action. Utilizing this rule over and over builds a bias toward action (fight response), which in turn leads to a pattern of action that is self-reinforcing. In other words, taking action leads to taking more action. So it's time to behave with the hope that your action will lead to success and to get out of your head and into the world to create the kind of life you know you actually want to design for yourself.

2. The key to overcoming the weak force of motivation is to shift toward an internal locus of control and to find a low enough risk activity that you will achieve the activation energy to attempt it. If you believe that you are in charge of your life, and you assign a small enough task to yourself that you will regularly attempt it, you're well on your way to reprogramming your brain.

3. When you do something small and get a dopamine hit for it, it trains your brain to seek dopamine from a similar activity. Doing it over and over again builds a pattern of behavior. Making the conscious choice (five … four … three … two … one) to produce the activation energy required to attempt bigger things more repetitively is called discipline.

4. You will fail from time to time, but it's better to try and occasionally fail than to never try at all. Your life is a steerable ship. You can start heading in a direction and alter your course if you want after a little way. Spartans swim new waters and attempt new things instead of imagining new waters and dreaming of new things.

Defining Moments

1. Do the workout at the beginning of this chapter.
2. Write and publish an article on your work.
3. Write down a goal that will take at least a year to complete—then complete it.
4. Remember a time when you felt that the world had treated you unfairly and exercise an internal locus of control in rewriting that memory for yourself.
5. Start an initiative at work with only 80 percent of the information you think you need.
6. Pick up a goal you have given up on and finish it.

Questions for Consideration

1. Do you have an internal or external locus of control bias?
2. What are your major goals for this year?

3. What daily or weekly disciplines will you begin to achieve your goals?

4. Who on your team is motivated by carrots and sticks? Can you shift them toward being intrinsically motivated just by refocusing them on their personal goals?

5. Are you action oriented or thinking oriented?

Pillar 4

Make Eye Contact

MiniSpartan Workout
This is a partner workout, so you'll need to recruit someone to do it with you.

Warmup
Each of you will do 2 rounds of:
  10 air squats
  10 jumping jacks
  10 pushups

Workout
160 kettlebell swings: 12 kg (26 lb.) male and 8 kg (18 lb.) female
  80 box jumps (24″)
  50 burpees
  2 km (1.25-mile) run

You will share this workload with someone else. One of you is always working while the other is resting. Only one works at a time. You may do any of the four exercises in any order. You can split the work into as many sets and reps per set as you like. But all of it must be completed as quickly as you can, so start a timer and then *go!*

Cooldown
200 m (0.2 mile) walking
10 mins stretching

Spartan Workout
This is a partner workout, so you'll need to recruit someone to do it with you.

Warmup
Each of you will do:
20 air squats
20 m bear crawls
20 jumping jacks
20 pushups

Workout
300 kettlebell swing: 20 kg (44 lb.) male/12 kg (26 lb.) female
150 box jumps (24")
80 burpees
4 km (2.5-mile) run

You will share this workload with someone else. One of you is always working while the other is resting. Only one works at a time. You may do any of the four exercises in any order. You can split the work into as many sets and reps per set as you like. But all of it must be completed as quickly as you can, so start a timer and then *go*!

Cooldown
200 m (0.2-mile) walking
10 minutes stretching (concentrate on your hamstrings—they're gonna hurt)

This workout will teach you the value of having someone with you to carry a heavy load and accomplish things that would be nearly impossible on your own. Of course, you can probably do it by yourself, but two of you together can do it in less than half the time that it would take you to do it alone. You can do more when you have the right people with you, focused on the same task and sharing the workload.

Tough Mudder

A year after my first Spartan race, I had developed a bit of a passion for obstacle course racing. I had already raced a Desert Warrior Challenge, a NAS Night Challenge, and another Spartan sprint. Then a friend asked me if I was running the Tough Mudder. "Of course," I said and then immediately Googled it to find out what it was.

The first Tough Mudder in the UAE was in 2016. I was there jumping and cheering with about 50 other people starting at the same time. It was a 16 km (10-mile) race, most of it in soft sand, so a real calf killer. I was doing well, trudging through the mud, climbing over the walls, running up and down in the sand. It was all going great until I arrived at the Block Ness Monster.

I jumped into a pool of mud that covered me to my chest and reached out to jump up and grab onto a massive block protruding from the water. I jumped up and easily grabbed the lip of the block to climb up onto it, but then something very discouraging happened. It rotated. The block that I was clearly supposed to climb over rotated in my direction when I pulled on it, and I fell back into the mud.

That's when I learned that if I was going to finish this race, I was going to have to make eye contact.

I looked around, and another runner jumped into the water beside me. And then another behind him. I looked at them both; they had seen me slide back, so we all knew what needed to be done. I said, "You first!" He immediately jumped up and grabbed the edge of the block, while the other guy and I braced the bottom of the block to keep it from turning. We pushed up and forced the block to rotate, with our new friend on it, to get him over the top and onto the other side.

The next guy went. I braced the block and pushed, and the guy who went first jumped up on the other side to use his body weight to pull and get the block rotating. Then the two of them jumped up on the other side, with me holding on, and their body weight rotated the block and easily pulled me over.

Not only could I not do it alone, but the only way for me to do it was to let two other guys do it for me. It was a bit unnerving, and fun to figure out, and made us feel a little vulnerable. But we got used to it quickly. There were three of those blocks in a row, and once we had solved the first, we helped each other over the next two.

But then something remarkable happened. Did I continue running at my pace, alone, as I would have in any other race? No. We ran together, the three of us. All strangers. We had learned that this was not the kind of race we would be able to finish alone, and so we became a team. Just like that.

We stuck together after that and all ran at the same pace. We had bonded and recognized the limitations of running this particular race alone. Sure enough, after about 500 meters, there was another huge obstacle that we all needed each other to complete. A couple of kilometers after that, there was the Pyramid Scheme.

It's a steep slope up, the height of four people standing on each other's shoulders. With all the mud and water on the ramp, and a muddy water pit at the bottom, it's very slippery. One person alone can stand on the edge and reach up, but it's impossible to climb, run to the top, or jump to the top. So the three of us on our new rookie team stood there, puzzled. We realized that we needed one person at the bottom and others climbing up our bodies to stand on our shoulders, until, ultimately, the fourth person on our team would be able to reach the top, at which time the person at the bottom could climb up the human ladder we had built, and thereby we could all reach the top, each person pulling the others up to the top of the wall.

Except for one thing. There were only three of us.

You guessed it! Eye contact time. We didn't even have to say it out loud. We just looked around for other teams that were too small to do it on their own and made awkward and pleading eye contact with them until, after a minute, we found a couple of freelancers looking for us as well. We partnered up.

I offered to go on the bottom, and before long, a stranger whose name I hadn't even asked had a foot on my hip and another on my shoulder as he climbed me to get up. Then he stood on my shoulders, leaning against the ramp, while another stranger climbed us both to make the ladder higher. Once we had four in a row, we could reach the top, and the five of us together were able to climb up our human ladder, stepping on each other's backs, heads, shoulders, and prides, to get to the top as a team. At the top, we all gave each other a big high-five and kept going. But did we separate into two and three again? Nope. This was not the kind of race we could run alone.

A while later, we were face to face with Everest, a massive four-meter-high quarter pipe, slippery as usual, with a small lip at the top to grab onto and pull yourself up. The curve made it impossible to build the same human ladder that we had built for the Pyramid Scheme, so we needed a new approach.

One all-star runner would need to get to the top and then reach down to help the rest of the team, one at a time, who would take turns running up the ramp to grab the leader's hand. Each person would get pulled up by one or more team members already at the top of the obstacle. So ... all-star runner, you say? I said I'd give it a shot.

I backed up about 20 meters and sprinted as fast as I could toward the ramp. I gave it absolutely all my power, not wanting to embarrass myself in front of my new teammates, who were all cheering for me and clapping. About halfway up the ramp, I took a leap of faith and stretched out my hand to catch the lip at the top—and missed by a full forearm length, smashing my face into the ramp and slowly sliding, like a deflated meat balloon, to the bottom.

The condolences were swift. "Good try, buddy" and "Yeah, dude, you were close." And my favorite: "You'll get it next time for sure."

WTF?

"What next time? I'm done."

"C'mon, man, you've got the speed. Just take one more step before you leap and you'll make it."

So I gathered myself up, walked back the 20 meters, and decided that I needed to do this. For me, for my country, my family, for the Insta, and for my new teammates who were counting on me, even though I didn't know any of their names.

I sprinted again, taking longer strides this time and an extra one before the leap. Stretching out my hand with everything I had, I imagined myself as Indiana Jones, reaching out for the edge of a cliff after leaping off of a collapsing bridge.

I hooked on, and the cheers drowned out my shock that I had actually done it. I pulled myself up, and without even considering the alternatives, I turned back to the team, dropped to my stomach, and reached my hand as far down the ramp as I could to cut down the leap for my teammates.

One by one, they ran and jumped, grabbing my hand, and we pulled them all up to the top of the ramp as a team. Another round of high-fives! Then we were running again—as a team.

There were also a number of ten-foot vertical walls that cannot be scaled unless you have someone else to stand on. And so it goes. The Tough Mudder, unlike the Spartan, cannot be completed alone. So you can imagine my surprise, having entered the event alone, to learn that I could not, even at my best, complete it without making eye contact. I had to connect with people on the course and convince these strangers to help me. The only way I could do that was by helping them in kind. I noticed a few things in the process.

First, I had to be humble enough to ask strangers for help. I had to admit to myself that I could not do it alone, and having no team with me, I needed to join another one. It was slower because I couldn't run at my own pace. I had to run at the pace of the team. But people were willing to help me. They reached their hands out to pull me up. I stood on their shoulders, and they stood on mine. It was all very natural, not awkward at all, and often led to a good laugh along the way.

Second, I enjoyed helping others. I could make the initial run up the Everest and reach the top on my own. But once I was there, my instinct wasn't to abandon my team of strangers and continue my race; it was to turn around, lie down on top of the ramp, reach out my hand, and pull up those who couldn't make the leap without the extra help. *My* help. All-star leaders also aren't known for how fast they climbed the ladder or how high they jumped alone but for how many people they pulled up behind them.

Third, other Spartans had joined the course but completely missed the point. From time to time, some solo runner would approach and climb up me or one of my teammates, complete the obstacle with my help, and continue running. This happened twice, and I noticed that my respect for those who ran the Tough Mudder like a Spartan was really low. In fact, I despised them; we all did. They used me, and others around me, for their own gain. They may have been fast and strong, but I didn't respect them. They may have finished the race eventually, but they finished alone. And this is not the kind of race you can run alone.

Too often, bosses think of themselves like Spartans in a Tough Mudder race, running a course of challenges, using people along the way to accomplish things that they alone take credit for but could not have possibly achieved without the help of others. They take credit for the win and ignore the team that made it possible, a team that, more often than not, despises and disrespects them behind their backs.

What we need in our leaders is Tough Mudders that run Spartan races. We need leaders who will lift others up, slow down and reach back to make sure the team stays together, and use their strength and speed to set a pace that keeps the team moving without leaving members behind. The natural instinct to help others is the same in business as it is on the obstacle course. Good bosses ask for help and reach back to offer it to others, and bad bosses stand on the shoulders of their people in order to run faster alone and finish without either respect or admiration.

You can't run the Tough Mudder like a Spartan, but you can definitely run the Spartan like a Tough Mudder. In many of my subsequent Spartan races, I assembled a team to run with. It might have slowed me down a bit, but that's the trade-off for having the help of others to complete the challenge, and it's a small price to pay for the laughter earned along the way.

How We All Became Teams

The human race has been around for more than 300,000 years, give or take. For most of that time, we've known that strict individualism is fatal among humans. We have two primary drives: survive and reproduce. Every decision we make is founded on those two evolutionary mandates. It's possible to do one of them alone but not the other. Traditionally, a male human would need to partner with a female human to have little humans together. The most effective strategy for them both to pass their genes on to the next generation was to partner together to provide for and protect their young.

But having offspring is an intensely costly investment for humans. Babies take nine months to gestate, which makes survival extremely difficult for pregnant female humans, who need to eat more, are much less able to hunt and gather for themselves, and become much more vulnerable to mortal threats during pregnancy and in early postnatal months. Not only that, but very young humans are in need of constant care and protection for a period lasting years. A mother without another adult partner was not only in danger herself but also, through her reduced ability to provide for and protect herself, was often in a restricted position to provide for her offspring.

So if humans wanted to procreate, the most effective way was to partner up, for female humans especially. Those humans whose

genes were successfully passed to the next generation predominantly did so through mothers who had the ability to survive
both the pregnancy process and the weaning years. This was
the imperative behind what psychologists call pair bonding. She
could protect and care for the children, while he hunted and gathered enough for all of them to eat. They did this until the children
were old enough to survive on their own. Bonded humans had
a better chance of survival and successful procreation (Morris,
1967).

A family was stronger than an individual and gave the offspring
a better chance of survival. But two families together were even
stronger than one. One male could protect both families, while
the second male hunted enough to feed all of them. If they added
a third family to the tribe, then one male could gather, one could
hunt, and one could protect, and the women could share the bur-
den of rearing the children and also help in the hunting and gathering. Those better at hunting became hunters, those better at
gathering became farmers, and those better at protection eventually became the military, police officers, and security guards.
Specialization of labor was born out of a dominant efficiency:
humans survive in bonded tribes, with tribal identity that gave
them a sense of belonging to each other. It has variously been
called tribal identity, nationality, and, in more recent times, corporate culture.

In ancient times, tribal members could work to provide for and
protect each other, with the adult humans specializing in specific labor roles. But the tribe had another effective way to gather
resources: they could take them by force from other tribes. Armed
with weapons, a tribe could assign its strongest members to

attack and steal from another weaker tribe, which both supplied the attacking tribe with more resources and made it more difficult for the defeated tribe to survive and compete for limited territorial resources. Fast forward a few thousand years, and we have kings of countries attacking other countries to dominate land and resources. This is the way it went until the industrial revolution.

In the eighteenth century, we accelerated the current shift from military to economic war. Families are still families, but tribes are now called companies, and countries are slowly turning into multinational corporations. Allegiances are increasingly built on economic projects rather than geographical territories. The black lines drawn on world maps matter less and less with each passing generation as the powerful economies of the world are shifting from being territorial and political kingdoms to market-based and economic communities.

Now, instead of hunters, gatherers, caretakers, and warriors, we have digital marketing analysts, Six Sigma Blackbelt process engineers, lighting designers, chief legal officers, forklift drivers, and radiologists. My point is we have a lot more specializations now, and our tribes are composed differently. The principles of warfare for the control of resources is still at play, but it's a more elegant game. We don't throw spears at each other's heads anymore; it's an uncivilized way to compete for resources (Pinker, 2011).

Now that we live in a more civilized age, our wars are carried out in economic fields as we compete for the resources of the market. It's still tribe versus tribe, community versus community, but it's economic tribes and communities at war now. Instead of facing each other head-on in battle, we face each other indirectly through an ongoing system of third-party arbitrations that judge where the resources should go. A purchaser, whether as an end consumer or on behalf of another community, looks at the products and services offered by a number of communities and chooses from among them. Once a selection is made, resources flow in the direction of the winning community. That's economic war. It's an elegant game. It's elegant enough to have regulators and procurement policies as referees for fair play.

So you have a couple of options as a human in the world these days. You can go out and hunt and gather for yourself, like the freegans or the Mountain Men, or you can join forces with representatives of other families offering specialized services to epic economic games, like the automotive game, the FMCG (Fast Moving Consumer Goods) game, or the tech game. In these economic games, the specialized resources of every tribal member are combined for the ultimate benefit of the tribe.

Alliances, mergers, acquisitions, joint ventures, and exclusivity agreements are all examples of how economic tribes agree to work together for mutual benefit and improved economic competition. But no company in history has ever made a deal with another company. Companies don't exist in the sense that they are independent entities. They are collections of representatives. Every deal in history has been made by one or more representatives of a community with one or more representatives of another community. At its very core, business still requires human-to-human bonding, which we as humans know instinctively is driven by eye contact.

Leonidas, the king of Sparta, after whom this book was named, is most famous for his heroic defense of the Pass of Thermopylae against the invading King Xerxes in 480 BCE. The movies tell the story of a fearless warrior king leading his army of 300 Spartans to meet a Persian army of between 70,000 and 300,000 warriors. What doesn't often make the final cut of the story is the fact that in addition to the 300 Spartans that Leonidas brought with him, he had an extra 6,000+ fighters from supporting armies. He was an accomplished diplomat as well.

Okay, 7,000-ish fighters versus a quarter-million Persians is still a losing battle, and, yes, Leonidas was courageous (if not a bit foolhardy) to march his tiny army into such an off-balanced fight. The point is he didn't go alone, and he didn't only take his own team with him. He enlisted the help of other teams.

After Leonidas was betrayed by Ephialtes and the Persian army eliminated the tactical advantage at the Pass of Thermopylae, Leonidas inspired his Spartans to continue fighting. The majority of the Greek army retreated, but the Spartans stayed to inflict as much damage on the Persians as possible before their inevitable defeat. Even then, Leonidas was not alone. He had his 300 best with him and about 1,100 more Boeotians besides that. Even then, in the end, facing impossible odds, Leonidas made eye contact.

The most effective strategy in business is still the same one that humans have honed over 300,000 years of evolution: find other humans that you trust and work together. The trust strategy is predominantly governed by the neurochemical oxytocin. It's behind hiring decisions, contracts, and humans who choose to work into the wee hours of the morning, when no one is looking, to finish a proposal on behalf of their economic community so that they can win the next battle for the approval of the market. Oxytocin is the most valuable currency on the planet.

All We Need Is Oxytocin

The glue that binds humans together in relationships is called oxytocin. It's produced in the hypothalamus of the brain and is best known for its role in initiating the childbirth process and milk production during the final stages of pregnancy. However, it's not reserved for child-bearing humans; it's a major player in all human relationships. In popular literature, it's sometimes called the love hormone or the trust hormone—and for good reason. Those are its day-to-day functions: love and trust.

Oxytocin is a lot stronger in romantic couples than in unattached singles, and its presence early in a romantic relationship aids in its longevity (Scheele et al., 2012; Schneiderman, Zagoory-Sharon, Leckman, & Feldman, 2012). Since partner relationships need to last longer as they put both members into positions of vulnerability (being physically vulnerable, sharing resources, protecting offspring, etc.), oxytocin helps humans know who they can trust in the long term. But it also works quickly so that we can know who to trust with nearly immediate effect, in less than 0.2 seconds according to one study (Ortigue, Bianchi-Demicheli, Patel, Frum, & Lewis, 2010).

To survive, humans had to develop ways to create trust between each other in seconds, so these are hardwired into our brains (Hamrick, Lum, & Ullman, 2018). When faced with a stranger, we need to be able to determine very quickly if they pose a threat to us, and if our desire is not to pose a threat to them, we need a very quick way to produce a neurochemical response in their brain that lowers their stress and suspicion and creates an opportunity for us to work together. It's a tool you use in everyday life, and since more than half of your life is your work, you use it at work too.

Oxytocin produces not only trust but also empathy, positive communication, loyalty, relaxation, and psychological stability, and it even helps us to remember things in a more positive light (Neumann, 2007; Wudarczyk, Earp, Guastella, & Savulescu, 2013). Synthetic oxytocin has been used as a treatment for antisocial psychological disorders such as autism (Parker, 2017). In one study, oxytocin also had the effect of making people 80 percent more generous (Zak, Stanton, & Ahmadi, 2007). So as a rule of thumb, friendly, trusting, generous people produce more oxytocin than unfriendly, untrusting, stingy people.

Trust and distrust are governed in entirely separate parts of the brain. Trust is in the prefrontal cortex, producing oxytocin in the hypothalamus. But the prefrontal cortex is a fairly new part of the human brain, from an evolutionary perspective. Distrust, in contrast, is housed in the amygdala, the primitive brain, and it is signaled by vasopressin and produces cortisol. Although vasopressin is associated with distrust in the brain, cortisol is in many ways the opposite of oxytocin in terms of its outcomes. Cortisol is more instant and more dominant than oxytocin. It's our stress hormone, designed to help us respond to threats and risks, often released with adrenaline in a fight, flight, or freeze response. These highlight the negative responses produced by a lack of trust.

In contrast, oxytocin is a low-stress response, from a neuro-chemical perspective. It can only be produced when you already feel safe and connected, when you're with someone who has your back and who is trusting you to have theirs. So not only is it safe to say that friendly, trusting people produce more oxytocin but also that they're less stressed and that stress-filled people may be so as a result of a lack of human connection and stable relationships.

Remember, half of your life is spent in relationships with people you work with, so instability and distrust there are major concerns. Being connected helps you to relax, be more positive, be more psychologically stable, and withstand more stress triggers without stressing out.

The alternative is cortisol, which, in addition to a lot of other really bad side effects, is a major contributor to weight gain. Cortisol is great at helping you to identify risk and manage stress, in part by telling your metabolism to slow down so that you conserve more energy. But too much cortisol leads to fatigue, distraction, weakness, headaches, and high blood pressure.

Oxytocin and cortisol are neurological opponents; they mitigate each other, and both are there to help you survive, one by improving collaboration with other humans and the other by identifying potential risk of danger or harm in other humans. But we live in more peaceful times now than we ever have before, and our well-developed cortisol production system is largely unnecessary in a world where people aren't trying to kill us in our sleep and we can eat more than once a day. I'm not saying that cortisol is outdated, just that it's less necessary than it used to be in terms of ensuring our survival. So if there was a way to choose oxytocin over cortisol, would you? And what if you could influence that choice for others as well?

Connecting with Others

Okay, so cortisol is a dominant, fast-acting stress hormone that propels us into weight gain through trigger-happy fight, flight, or freeze responses. To make matters worse, since we're not being chased by neighboring tribespeople with spears anymore, cortisol is produced in modern times by even minor stressors like not getting enough engagement on social media, or not getting a response on WhatsApp for more than 30 minutes, or the restaurant not having the dessert we went there specifically to order. It's super lame.

As for oxytocin, yes, you can produce it on your own as well, though that approach is not as much fun. Essentially, this happens when you connect with others all by yourself, in your head. It's a social chemical, so there needs to be another human involved, even if it's all in your mind. There are two basic brain hacks for this. First, thinking about someone you're fond of produces oxytocin. The brain can't tell the difference between what it sees and what it imagines, so if you close your eyes and think about a person you feel connected to, then your brain will begin to produce oxytocin. It's also important to note that oxytocin is not produced just by feeling joy or satisfaction. Feeling good and feeling oxytocin good are two different things (Algoe & Way, 2014).

Second, you can produce it by being grateful. Gratitude produces oxytocin (Algoe & Way, 2014). This is especially helpful when you are angry. Anger is a fight response to a real or perceived threat; it produces cortisol and adrenaline in the brain. So if you're angry and you want to counteract that cocktail of adrenaline and cortisol, you can be grateful. Gratitude is the antidote for anger. It's neurochemically impossible for humans to remain angry and grateful at the same time. Seriously, try it. Try to think of something that you're really angry about and then think of something you're grateful for. What happens to the anger? It doesn't work. Cool, right? Since gratitude is an act of will from the prefrontal cortex, the primitive anger response will subside and give way to it. Okay, I agree that it's a challenging thing to be grateful when you're angry, but, anyway, there you have it. The cure for anger is gratitude.

Eye Contact
The eyes are the window to the soul, and being oxytocin fit requires eye contact. The faster you make eye contact, the more quickly you'll be recognized and more positively you'll be assessed. One study calls it the "eye contact effect" (Senju & Johnson, 2009). Conversely, when you refuse eye contact, it communicates that you do not value the connection or relationship. Think about conversations you've had with people who make good eye contact and those who don't. Which do you prefer? Which makes you feel valued and heard?

If you make eye contact for less than a second, it can communicate that you are avoiding the other person. But there's such a thing as too much eye contact as well. If you make eye contact for more than 10 seconds, it is likely to indicate that you are interested in the other person sexually or that you want to start a fight with that person, depending on if your other facial microexpressions are communicating favor or disfavor. One study had strangers of the opposite sex stare into each other's eyes for two minutes and found that they predominantly felt increased feelings of love and affection for those they were looking at (Kellerman, Lewis, & Laird, 1989). This kind of eye gazing actually synchronizes the parts of both people's brains that are associated with socialization and empathy (Koike et al., 2015).

A study that set out to measure the ideal length of eye contact between humans found that the optimal length is between two and five seconds, with no one preferring less than one second or more than nine (Binetti, Harrison, Coutrot, Johnston, & Mareschal, 2016). So what happens neurochemically when you make eye contact for between two and five seconds? Well, not only does it produce more oxytocin, but the reverse is true as well: ingesting synthetic oxytocin increases eye contact (Macdonald & Macdonald, 2010). If you're not having a fight, you're neurochemically building trust, and if you keep staring long enough, you might even fall in love (careful).

Conversational Intelligence

There are practical ways to build trust through word choices in conversations too, but the most powerful of them is none of them. Listening is almost a lost art among most managers and leaders. As a rule of thumb, if you want to build trust with someone, you should aim to spend 70 percent of your conversational time listening. People tend to feel the conversation went well if they spent the majority of the time talking. It requires a conscious choice to decide that the conversation went well even though you spent the majority of your time listening.

There are certain word choices that you are listening for as well to determine whether people are in a state of self-protection or a state of collaboration. If they say "I" instead of "we," then they are likely to be in a state of self-preservation. When they switch to "we," then you have reached a collaborative state, and they are more likely to be producing oxytocin in their brains (Glaser, 2014).

Also, try asking questions that you don't have answers to. We often ask questions for which we have already presupposed answers in our heads. We do that because being right about the answer gives us a sense of control over the world and a hit of dopamine for being right. If you ask questions you genuinely don't have answers for, then you are relying on your curiosity and their honesty. It's an opportunity to build trust.

Glaser's (2014) research has shown that three of the best ways to produce oxytocin in someone you're talking to are to:

1. be truthful about what's on your mind
2. paint a picture of mutual success
3. express concern for others

Three of the best ways to kill oxytocin in the conversation are to:

1. focus on convincing others of something
2. pretend to be listening
3. not understand the other person

People need to be listened to. In fact, most people are okay with being overruled or disagreed with as long as they feel heard and understood. Feeling heard and understood helps us to validate that the community we are investing in values our contributions, even if they aren't being used as often as we would prefer.

Appropriate Touch

We, humans, are civilized animals, and we generally only allow people to touch us once we already consider them not a threat. So touching someone who doesn't expect it or doesn't want it will produce cortisol immediately and might provoke a fight response that you don't want. However, if you already have some level of relationship, then a handshake, hug, or hand on the shoulder is likely to produce oxytocin both in yourself and others. Affectionate touch is a bonding behavior in humans. It's a fast way to oxytocin.

Did you know that there are professional cuddlers? A quick Google search will reveal several platforms and blogs of professionals who provide cuddles for a fee. It's not sexual, so why do people pay for cuddles? It's a quick way to produce oxytocin. An extended touch from someone trusted helps humans to feel protected, cared for, and safe. That sense of security is a prerequisite for oxytocin production.

Context is also important. Let's face it: I don't think I would have smiled kindly if a stranger on the street suddenly jumped on my back, climbed up my shoulders, and stepped on my head to reach something. Yet in the Tough Mudder, that was considered acceptable and appropriate touch between strangers who had made eye contact but still didn't know each other's names. Environment and context are strong considerations. Do you remember the guy who ran the Tough Mudder like a Spartan, running up my back and carrying on all by himself? Why is it acceptable for one person to use me like that and not another? What was the difference? Eye contact. Unlike my team members, the Spartan runner was alone, stayed alone, and didn't make enough eye contact with me to justify his touch as appropriate. There was no oxytocin.

Performance without Management

There's a lot of material on performance management in the business disciplines. It's a huge scientific field now, the general inquiry of which is how to get people to perform at their best. But what if peak performance could not be achieved through management at all? What if the activities traditionally associated with management (monitoring, KPIs, targets, etc.) actually impeded peak performance by replacing real relationships with mechanistic proxies like performance review meetings? What if performance management is an oxymoron? Most of our behaviors as humans are governed by the need to define and protect our social structure by determining who in our social circles are real or potential members of our personal tribe of stakeholders (Baumeister, Brewer, Tice, & Twenge, 2007).

So if most of our behaviors are driven by the need to belong in society, what if we as leaders respected that wiring and started to treat humans like humans instead of as resources? What if people weren't pieces of a puzzle or cogs in a well-oiled machine, but rather they were members of economic tribes called companies who competed for resources on the planet in peaceful and elaborate economic games? Not machine parts, not resources but players on a team in a global competition for resources.

Humans in relationships, the same way we've been doing it for 300,000 years.

What do all humans want? At the top of the list are dopamine, oxytocin, and serotonin (another happiness-related neurochemical). All humans want these things all of the time, and they will bend their lives around finding reliable sources of them. Monetary rewards for good performance are interesting extrinsic motivators but ultimately weak from an evolutionary psychological perspective. Money is a proxy reward; it's a placeholder for food, security, and outsourced protection. Humans aren't wired to seek money; the lust for money is actually a mask for the insecurity that comes from the feeling of not having a strong tribe able to provide one with enough food, shelter, water, healthcare, domain, etc. Those are the real human needs. Money is a weak proxy.

Oxytocin is not a proxy. It's a major and direct priority on the human desires list. Humans don't desire oxytocin as a proxy for relationship; they desire oxytocin because it *is* relationship, from a neurochemical standpoint. It is the only way we measure provision, protection, social inclusion, honor, value, and social meaning. Oxytocin feeds our core wiring for defining ourselves as humans. Ensuring that we are surrounded by other humans we can trust is the single most dominant activity in our lives. Not convinced? Check Facebook.

Finding friends is the core function of about 80 percent of our neurogenetic makeup (Baumeister & Leary, 1995). We all need each other. And for Spartan leaders who are paying attention right now, the oxytocin that governs that fundamental human need … well, it's free. No budget line.

As one researcher put it,

> Humans are relationship-forming animals who are programmed to make decisions on the basis of what will deepen existing supportive relationships or create new ones ... We are motivated to perform at a higher level because of our commitment to the relationship with our manager, or to strengthen the bonds with the other members of the group we work with and to ensure that group's survival. (Murray, 2015)

Humans will accept lower pay in order to work in a meaningful job where they feel connected with the people around them and the work that they're doing. How much lower pay? Twenty-three percent lower.

Not 23 percent lower than their current salary, mind you. Twenty-three percent lower lifetime earnings. That's how much people value relationships at work. A study of 2,285 professionals across 26 industries revealed that 9 out of 10 humans will forego 23 percent of all future earnings in order to have meaningful connections at work (BetterUp, 2017). Considering that people on average spend 21 percent on their housing costs, that makes meaningful work more valuable than shelter, from a psychological perspective

There's your budget line.

The same study found that employees who are connected with their work take two fewer leave days per year, work an extra hour each week, and last 7.4 months longer in the company. Not only do they work more, but they're more productive too. They're more likely to receive a raise, more likely to receive a promotion, and 28 percent less likely to be planning their exit. So when you calculate those productivity benefits (Böckerman & Ilmakunnas, 2012), you end up with an average value of about USD $9,078 per worker in benefits to the company (Achor, Reece, Kellerman, & Robichaux, 2018).

Oxytocin governs the human sense of belonging, and belonging governs our behaviors when no one is looking, and that's where the margin of your company really lies. Your margin lies in what your people are doing when they aren't being managed. So you see? Real performance isn't managed at all. It can't be. Real performance can't be governed by programs, cameras, training, or reviews. What people do when they're not being managed is entirely up to them, and they can be either adding to or removing from the resources of the organization. The social ties that bind us to each other are what keep us loyal to each other when no one is looking. Oxytocin is correlated to loyalty, and, again, that's where your margin is.

Equal Is Not the Same
Oxytocin is the chemical formula for trust and loyalty among humans, and both male and female humans value loyalty above any other trait when choosing a romantic partner (Emond & Eduljee, 2014). It's not out of line to expect the same from humans partnering with each other for economic purposes, especially since economic safety and security are at the foundation of our hierarchy of needs. All humans value loyalty above all else

in relationships, and loyalty from a psychological perspective is driven by oxytocin from a neurochemical perspective.

However, the neurobiology and neurochemistry of male and female brains are not the same. During gestation and adolescence, significant changes take place that drive male and female brains further apart in terms of physical and chemical composition. For example, although males have bigger brains, female brains are larger relative to their size. Females also have relatively more gray matter in their brains (Cahill, 2006; Peper & Koolschijn, 2012).

Females have overall more connections between the right and left halves of their brains than males, and males have overall more connections within the right and left sides of their brains than females (Ingalhalikar et al., 2014). "A behavioral component of the study found that these differences allowed females to significantly outperform males on face memory, word, attention, and social cognition tests, while males performed better than females on motor speed and spatial processing tests" (Ryan, 2017). Males and females even use different parts of their brains to complete the exact same cognitive tasks.

Male and female humans may be equal, but we are definitely not the same. The reason I bring this up here is that in the oxytocin game, for example, female humans have a clear advantage.

Females have a higher baseline of oxytocin and more oxytocin receptors than men (Zak, Boria, Matzner, & Kurzban, 2005), meaning their ability to feel the connection, loyalty, belonging, and meanings associated with oxytocin is much easier than for males. Males have more testosterone, and females have more estrogen hormones. Testosterone tends to suppress oxytocin, while estrogen tends to enhance it (Riedl & Javor, 2012). So not only do females produce more oxytocin, but they're better at incorporating it into their neurochemistry.

All that is to say that though we are politically equal, in terms of oxytocin and its benefits to the corporate community in which you work, having more females is a competitive advantage. In one of my current clients' companies, there are more female than male employees. It makes a huge difference. There's more connection, less politics, more cheering, and less internal competition. More oxytocin, less cortisol.

Trust at Work

So what do you do to build trust at work? That's what you're asking now, right? You're convinced that it's good for you and for those around you, so you're looking for ways to build it.

1. Encourage community applause. I often sign off on messages by saying "I'm cheering for you" because it causes people to think about me thinking about and encouraging them.
2. Measure happiness. I'm not kidding. Just asking people how happy they are at work will make them happier because someone cared enough to ask. Plus, if there are unhappy employees, you'll find them and be able to address their concerns.
3. Have a clearly articulated and meaningful vision, mission, and values statement. Humans need to know the

grand narratives around which they are orchestrating their lives. Meaningful corporate words are focal points for people to find personal meaning.

4. Oxytocin is the most valuable currency in business. It is trust. Your ability as a leader to build and maintain trust is the single greatest determiner of what your people will be doing when no one is looking, and it's in those moments when no one is looking that your profit margin sits. I'm not saying that you should connect with people *because* it's profitable; I'm saying that connecting with people *is* profitable. It's cash-in-the-bank profitable.

Spartan Core Finisher

1. You are *not* a hotshot maverick, lone wolf, A-type loner. Those types die alone and don't accomplish much of value. You are a member of a team, family, tribe, economic community, national community, social group, and perhaps all of them at once. Everyone can do this, and no one can do it alone.

2. Make eye contact but don't be creepy. Build trust by actually being interested in connecting with the people whose efforts you need to accomplish your goals.

3. Align yourself with people whose goals you want to put your effort into achieving.

4. Maintain gender balance in leadership positions organizationally.

5. Pursue fun as a critical success factor in your business.

Defining Moments

1. Complete an obstacle course race with your work team.
2. Your team stops using the term "I" and starts using the term "we" as dominant language.
3. You help a stranger do something, and he or she helps you in kind.
4. You have a happiness KPI weighted in your own performance review.
5. There are as many women as men in executive positions in your organization.

Questions for Consideration

1. Who are the people in your life whom you trust the most? Why?
2. Who are the people you trust most at work?
3. Do your teammates trust you?
4. How much trust exists in your relationships with your friends, spouse, children, neighbors?
5. Who are the seven people in your life you are counting on the most for your own survival?

Pillar 5

Rest Like a Boss

MiniSpartan Workout
Warmup
Sit cross-legged on the floor. Close your eyes. Breathe in for a count of 6 seconds, and breathe out for a count of 6 seconds. Do this 10 times.

Workout
1 hour of beginner's yoga (go to a class or use YouTube)
   20-minute daytime nap (not kidding)

Cooldown
Name 10 things that you are grateful for
   Time cap: 24 hours

Spartan Workout
Warmup
15 minutes of meditation/mindfulness

Workout
1 round of the following:
   1 hour of intermediate or advanced yin yoga (specifically yin yoga)

20-minute daytime nap
30 minutes of meditation/mindfulness
8 hours of uninterrupted sleep
Eat a meal alone for 30 minutes. No phone. No computer. No TV.
Time cap: 24 hours

For some reason, this is the workout that everyone who has read this says is the most impossible. I've told you to do 250 wallballs, and yet this—yoga and mindfulness—tends to be the most difficult for Spartans. You will do it. You will do it because Spartans know that to be ready for battle, they must be well-rested. Now quit your whining and get your tights on!

Broga Is a Thing

A few years ago, I blew out my left shoulder doing CrossFit. It was terrible. I had done an infinite number of thrusters for time during a workout one day and didn't really think anything of it. But I woke up the next morning and couldn't raise my arm up past 45 degrees, and I was in a lot of ambient pain. Three doctors later, the MRI showed that my bursa was badly swollen, and I had pulled or maybe torn my supraspinatus muscle. My doctor asked what I had been doing. I told him that an infinite number of thrusters for time was a standard workout in CrossFit now; I think it's called The Bitch or something like that. But he had me account for all the shoulder work I had done in the 10 days leading up to the injury:

wallballs
strict press
push press
overhead snatches
overhead squats
handstand pushups
dumbbell snatches
throwing my kid into the pool
bear complexes
deadlifts
thrusters

That about covered it. So, yeah, in hindsight, I had done a bit of shoulder work. He asked if I had noticed any pain at all. I had; a few days prior, I had noticed some pain after doing strict presses at my max-3 weight. I didn't think anything of it, so I just slept it off and carried on the next day. But that was it; that was my body telling me something was wrong. I missed the cue.

I did a bit of rehab and some slow lifting in the gym for a while. It took about six months before my shoulder felt good again. My doctor told me not to do CrossFit anymore. But what do doctors know anyway? After all, I'm a doctor (of sorts), and I'm faking it most of the time. Haha. So I went back to the box and started working out again. It was amazing. I felt great, and I resented the time I had to waste doing what felt like nothing while my stupid shoulder healed. I resented the loss of strength from not having done shoulder work for months. But now I was back, baby—back!

For three months.

And then I blew out my right shoulder. FML.

Same problem. Since my left side was damaged, I was using my right side to compensate and ended up with a weak left and fully injured right. This time, I was out of CrossFit for about a year. I worked on my endurance cardio with running and cycling and left my shoulders mostly rested. I humbled myself. I respected my shoulders and redefined my limits. The days of the 200 kg (440 lb.) deadlift were behind me permanently. I learned my lesson. And I learned to do yoga.

My first yoga class was about how you would expect. I could reach down to my ankles but not my toes. I couldn't get my head anywhere close to passing through my arms in a downward-facing dog. I had the grace and agility of a hippopotamus with an inner ear infection. Plus, I approached yoga with the same intensity that I approached CrossFit, so by the end of the hour, not only was I entirely fatigued from forcing myself into positions I hadn't been in since my days in the womb, but I was sloshing about in a puddle of sweat that ran off of my mat and onto the floor. I was the opposite of sexy, whatever that is.

The yogi approached me with a gracious and tolerant gaze. "Is this your first yoga class?"

"Yeah. I've never done anything like this before. It was really hard. Any pointers?"

"Breathe."

And with that, he gave me a big smile and walked away.

Breathe? What does that even mean? All I did was breathe! I was out of breath, for Pete's sake. Didn't he see me huffing and puffing, forcing my left heel behind my head with my eyes popping out and my skin turning a sunburnt Irishman's red? What a dick.

Or that's what I thought. So I decided to tackle the yoga problem with the same set of skills as I attack almost everything: research.

As it turns out, you need to breathe intentionally during yoga. Who knew? He wasn't a dick after all. In fact, you can't do the poses or movements properly unless you are able to override your subconscious breathing patterns and actually consciously choose to breathe and to not breathe. It took me a long time to learn to breathe. But after that, yoga became a bit more manageable. I learned to breathe in for six counts and out for six counts and to move my body in such a way that it rarely demanded more breath than I was choosing to provide. Sometimes I would still get into crazy positions that had me gasping for air, though. It happened more than I'd like to admit. But I'm a CrossFitter, after all, not a yogi.

It was also embarrassing. Doing yoga. A large, white male consultant in tight shorts and a sleeveless top, bending around and dripping with sweat, is about the least attractive thing I can imagine. Ick! But you know who's good at yoga? Girls. Girls are more bendy than sweaty white dudes, and my classes were full of them. They all seemed to be good at it. Balancing in perfect warrior-3 poses with straight backs and hinted, smirky faces when the odd one of them would glance over at the sweaty white guy quivering and wheezing, just a hair-trigger away from full-on panic. I'm sure I was a wonderful source of bendy-girl coffee fodder later in the day.

"Did you see that guy in the class today?"

"Gross, right? Like, not everyone can do yoga, y'know?"

"I dunno. When he fell over doing the headstand, that was funny. But at least he's trying."

"Maybe there should be a remedial yoga class for guys like that."

"Haha. Like, yeah."

But guess what? There was. There was a remedial class for guys like that ... like me. My gym had a yoga class for dudes called Broga. Not kidding. I started going there, and it was amazing. My first instructor was Carmen; she was really good-looking, so guys who went to yoga for the eye candy still got their fill, but other than that, it was a whole room full of sweaty, shaky dudes who bulged in all the wrong places and swore through their breath in the difficult holds.

It was hard to feel attracted to Carmen in that environment, though. She was really good at what she did, and a few guys made offside comments sometimes, which she tolerated with a smile, but for the most part, I just felt sorry for her. She was in a room with a dozen hippos doing ballet. It's about how I imagine professional dance instructors feel when they are working with toddlers. So far advanced from the class and yet with perfect patience to walk us through our bumbling attempts at a simple tree pose. You're my hero, Carmen, wherever you are.

The other benefits of Broga were the music and the swearing. It's not orthodox yoga, to be sure, but we would make rude or sarcastic comments, laugh, tell jokes, and swear during class. We also listened to the Red Hot Chili Peppers, Rage Against the Machine, Nirvana, and Blue October. It was great. I felt like I was with my people. And that's where I finally learned to breathe.

Failing at CrossFit taught me yoga. Failing at yoga taught me to breathe. Failing at breathing taught me mindfulness.

Choosing to breathe is really hard when you've never done it before. Breathing is normally involuntary, and I had been doing it without thinking for a long time. Humans take around 20,000 breaths each day, and I was over 40 before I tried yoga, so I had more than 290 million involuntary breaths under my belt. That's a lot of reps and a lot of muscle memory. I would have to do some unlearning before I learned something new.

Mindfulness is based on the same technology as meditation. It's self-control over body and mind in a relaxed state. I watched YouTube videos to learn how to do it, and it worked. I was slowly able to develop the skill of breathing. What had been instinct, akin to an involuntary twitch, I could control with a bit of foresight and focused awareness. This gave me better control over what was happening in my body and my mind. That's where Spartans will find an unexpected source of energy and clarity.

It was more than a year before I went back to CrossFit, but I'm grateful for the timeout. I'm grateful for yoga. And I'm grateful for finally learning how to breathe.

No Days Off

Working too hard and resting too little will kill you. You need balance. We all do. But that's not what our heroes on Instagram are saying. Work hard. Put in the hours. Lift more than you think you can. Pursue your dreams at all costs. But where is the rest? When will we have time to heal from all of this working, lifting, and pursuing? We are humans, after all. So what's the balance we need to strike?

Well, now I'm back in CrossFit, and I train, no days off, for at least two solid months per year: usually January, to pay for my gluttony over the Christmas holidays, and September, to pay for my gluttony over the summer. The best endurance coach in my gym is Ahmed Sabry. Sabry laughed at me once and told me it's really unhealthy to train with no days off, and I mostly agreed with him. It's unsustainable, right? Unless you're Mat Fraser, you're probably going to have to take rest days. The alternative is to just not push as hard, which is what I do. When I'm in a no-days-off cycle, I scale my weights down slightly and never pursue a max rep. I want to give my body just enough damage that one or two nights of sleep will be enough to repair it.

For average humans who are new to exercise, you should rest when you feel like you're in pain after a workout. Work hard three times a week to start with and have a rest day in between. Now, for Spartans who are used to training more often, how many rest days do we actually need?

None.

(Insert Sabry's shock and awe here.)

A pair of studies has shown that there was no difference in gains made by subjects who trained more sets on fewer days over those who trained fewer sets every day (Gomes, Franco, Nunes, & Orsatti, 2019; Yang et al., 2018). As long as the load is the same, the gain is the same with or without rest days. Fun fact: when a human body has adapted to the daily demand for physical work, that same body can heal most of the damage within about 24 hours. These findings support an earlier study that concluded:

> High-frequency (6× per week) resistance training does not seem to offer additional strength and hypertrophy benefits over lower frequency (3× per week) when volume and intensity are equated. Coaches and practitioners can therefore expect similar increases in strength and lean body mass with both 3 and 6 weekly sessions. (Colquhoun et al., 2018)

So as long as you're not pushing for max loads every day, you'll be just as fine with a no-days-off strategy as you would with a staggered-days strategy. Whether you're working out three or six days a week doesn't matter. What matters is your level of effort—and that you're getting enough food and sleep.

That's discipline. No days off requires the kind of decision making that's well beyond the scope of motivation, as discussed in Pillar 3. It is a strategic choice to place the locus of control squarely in the prefrontal cortex and protect the time and energy required to sustain the pace. Remember, motivation gets you to the starting line; discipline gets you to the finish line. No days off is a discipline. Just to test this out, I did 63 days of CrossFit in a row while writing this book.

No Nights Off

Whenever people tell me they're in the 5:00 a.m. club, I ask them when they go to bed. More often than not, I wake up at five to be in the gym by six and to work by seven-thirty, but to maintain this pace, my wife and I go to bed at around 9:30 p.m. When people, mostly guys (for whatever reason), tell me that they wake up at five and go to bed at midnight, I feel bad for them. They don't know what they're doing to themselves by depriving their bodies of sufficient sleep.

As it turns out, you can work out more often than you thought, but you also need a sufficient amount of sleep to manage the healing load associated with your exercise regime. A great metastudy of an array of research on this subject concluded that sleep and exercise have mutually beneficial effects on each other (Dolezal, Neufeld, Boland, Martin, & Cooper, 2017). Good sleep aids exercise, and good exercise aids sleep, both in quality and duration, and in both directions.

The rule of thumb, then, must be that if you aren't exercising, then you won't sleep as well as you could be, and if you're not sleeping well, then you won't be able to exercise as well as you could. I don't want to dwell on this since it seems like a no-brainer, so I'll end with the recommendation to get seven to eight hours of sleep every night and to treat minutes under the seven-hour mark as a mounting sleep-deficit position. They will have to be paid for later. Plus, women need about 20 minutes more of sleep each night than men (Horne, 2007). So those people who are in the 5:00 a.m. club and hit the gym every day might actually be caught in a subtle but very real downward spiral if they're not going to bed by 9:30 or 10:00 p.m. every night.

We can train with no days off, but what happens when we don't rest with the same level of discipline as we train? What happens when we don't sleep seven or more hours, no nights off?

The largest study conducted to date comes from Cornell University and covers more than 3 million nights of sleep across 30,000 people. The big takeaway: going to bed an hour earlier than normal won't improve your performance, but staying up an extra hour will most certainly hinder it. For every 1 percent of decreased performance after one sub-six-hour night, the second sub-six-hour night will cost you 4 percent. So let's say Ahmed comes to work after sleeping less than six hours, and he's 5 percent less effective at work that day. If the second night he again gets less than six hours of sleep, he'll be 20 percent less effective the next day. Plus, the cognitive deficiencies that Ahmed experiences after two consecutive sub-six-hour nights last for six days following, even if he "catches up" on sleep during the third night (Althoff, Horvitz, White, & Zeitzer, 2017). Sleep deficiency is compounded over time.

Night 1:   5 hours' sleep
Day 1:   1x less productive
Night 2:   5 hours' sleep
Day 2:   4x less productive
Night 3:   7 hours' sleep
Days 3–9: Slow incline back to average productivity

The most interesting quality of this sleep study is that it is all based on real-world data. The sleep data was pulled from wearable fitness trackers, and the performance data was based on those users' computer activities: searching for things online, typing things, clicking speed, etc. So there was no lab, no artificial environment that might skew the study. It also took into account caffeine intake that might have altered performance after sleep loss. The research was conducted by mathematicians, not physiologists. Cool, huh? A team of mathematicians is telling us what the effects of sleep are on performance. I love science. Super fun.

Did you know the human brain is the largest consumer of calories in the body? True story. And when you are awake, about 80 percent of your brain's energy goes to inputting and processing sensory data: what you hear, see, smell, touch, and taste. I mean think about this: you're looking at squiggles and dots on a piece of paper right now, and your brain has to capture the difference in light reflecting off of different points on that page to identify the squiggles and dots as patterns it has seen before. Then it puts those letter patterns together to solve word-pattern puzzles. The word patterns become pieces of sentences, which become pieces of concept puzzles. Once the puzzle is solved, it transmits the concepts to the prefrontal cortex, where you become aware of about seven concepts, or one minute's worth of information at any given time. Currently, you're not only aware of the squiggles and dots on the page but also of the pink elephant that they represent. Now you are seeing a pink elephant in your head. That's a lot of computational power. Most of that shuts down at night.

You'd think that when people are sleeping, the brain is operating at about 20 percent capacity then, but that's not the case at all. The brain is just as active when sleeping as it is when it's awake. But since your sensory data center is powered down for the night, what do you suppose your brain is doing with all of that 80 percent leftover energy?

Well, you still have to do things like breathe, digest, and pump blood, so a bit of brain power is used on the involuntary functions. It also still keeps one eye open (so to speak) where your senses are concerned. If there's a loud noise or a bright light while you're sleeping, your brain will wake you up to check it out. The neurochemical associated with sleep is melatonin. Your brain produces it when it knows it's time to shut down, often when it's dark and quiet. Light tends to prevent melatonin production, so Spartan pro tip: Don't look at your phone if you happen to wake up midsleep. The artificial light will signal to your brain that the sun's up, and melatonin production will stop. Keep the light off, and you'll find it much easier to fall back asleep.

Your brain also cleans up a lot of leftover toxins at night. Just like a dishwasher running quietly in the background, the cerebrospinal fluid flushes out the brain and cleans up excess proteins and toxins such as beta amyloid (Xie et al., 2013). Beta amyloid builds up when we're awake, and it gets flushed when we sleep, and not flushing it leads to a buildup of the stuff, which is associated with Alzheimer's. Not kidding. Sleep deprivation contributes to Alzheimer's.

Your brain is also sorting through the information that it took in that day. It builds associations with other concepts, patterns, memories, and emotions in a process called transcription. Think back to a time before you knew my name. You had no concept of me. Then, suddenly, you heard a rumor, read an ad, or I popped up in a Google search for crazy Canadian consultants. Just like that, you saw or heard my name for the first time, represented by some squiggles and dots on the screen or a pattern of waves in the air that vibrated your eardrum.

That night, you went to bed, and your brain took the tiny bit of information you had on me and started to build a neural network that would fire when you heard or read "Corrie Block" in succession. To remember those patterns and what they mean, your brain linked them to other similar concepts, names that sound the same, other Corries or Blocks you've met in the past, other Canadians or consultants you know or knew, how you felt about those people, and whether or not you trusted them. Maybe you read that I'm a doctor, so you built associations with other doctors or what the concept of "doctor" means to you, which may be positive or negative, depending on your history. All of that happened when you slept. Now, quite literally, I'm in your head, and I'll stay there so long as that set of neurons gets fired from time to time.

Corrie
Corrie Block
Dr. Corrie Block

Haha. Just messing with you. You have a Corrie Block pattern of neurons in your head now. Anyway, if you want revenge, just write a strongly worded review of this book online somewhere. Once I've read it, you'll be in my head too.

So what have we learned so far? We can train every day as long as we are getting sufficient sleep every night. Going to bed on time, so that you sleep enough, is a discipline. Rest is a discipline, necessary not just for physical healing but for psychological well-being as well. Spartans sleep seven or more hours a night, no nights off.

Brainwaves

The brain operates on five main frequency bands. The highest frequency is observed in long-term meditators and Buddhist monks. Gamma waves are between 32 and 100 Hz, in which the brain can run several processes at once. This is the brain's peak performance state. It's a heightened state of awareness and the state in which neurons are most easily generated in the frontal cortex, the area of the brain where most of your intelligence is based.

Operating on gamma frequencies helps us to remain fully aware of everything around us and process incredible amounts of data, like when you're in a crisis and it feels like time slows down. That's your brain processing mountains of data very quickly, which gives us the sensation that time is slower. You can produce this in a negative way by giving in to anxiety and stress or during a car accident. Stressed people are often processing too much data, especially negative data. But you can also produce gamma waves in a positive way through extended and deep meditation.

You're probably not in that state now. Reading books tends not to demand all of our capacity for awareness at once. You might be in a beta wave state, between 13 and 32 Hz. This is the normal operating frequency of the human brain when you're awake. You can make decisions, process input, learn something new, and focus on tasks and problems. This is the normal conscious state.

When you start to relax, you will move toward the alpha wave state. These were the first brainwaves detected, in 1929, between 8 and 13 Hz, when you feel physically and mentally relaxed, are headed toward sleep, or are feeling really creative. This is often the state of my brain during yoga, or when I'm writing poetry, or when my eyes are closed. It's fairly easy for most people to choose to shift from beta to alpha. Just close your eyes and slow your breathing down to six seconds in, six seconds out. You'll be there in no time.

If you slip entirely into a daydream, you might have found the theta wave state, between 4 and 8 Hz. In this state, you'll be heavily relaxed. This is the state of deep meditation and shallow sleep, the dream state. This is also the state that your brain can slip into when you're doing something that's second nature to you, like brushing your teeth. You do it with great skill but without really being conscious of it.

The slowest brainwaves are delta, from 0.5 to 4 Hz. This is when you are in a dreamless sleep. In this state, your body can heal, and your mind can clean out toxins and sort through information at peak performance. This is the state in which the supermarket of your mind is closed so the janitors can mop up the messes, the maintenance crew can repair damaged facilities, and the stock people can fill up the shelves for the next day's demands. Don't turn on the lights too soon, or you're likely to go through a day with exposed wires, half-full shelves of information, and aisles blocked up by beta amyloid spills from the day before.

Delta	Theta	Alpha	Beta	Gamma
• 0.5–4 Hz	• 4–8 Hz	• 8–13 Hz	• 13–32 Hz	• 32–100 Hz
• Healing	• Daydreaming	• Relaxation	• Normal Operation	• Hyperfocused

Work as Rest: Flow

Somewhere between alpha and theta, at about the 8 Hz marker, you'll find what researchers call the flow state. This is when you are doing something that requires consciousness but not as much prefrontal awareness. You are aware but somewhere between relaxed and daydreaming. Have you ever been driving home and "woke up" along the way somewhere, or pulled into your parking spot without any memory of having driven there? You were always conscious, but you were much less aware. Yep, that's the state of flow. Here, your work is almost effortless.

I can get there if I have triphop music playing on my headphones and I'm doing research. I've done so much reading and writing in my life that I can often bring the information in and process it with reduced acute awareness of what I'm doing. In a state between alpha and theta, my mind is able to process lots of information with great efficiency, and it has better access to the creative centers of my brain. I can write for an extended period of time without having to be aware of anything else in the room.

My first wife used to drop me off at the library when I was researching for my master's degree in leadership. I could sit there in the same chair for eight or nine hours without standing up, going to the bathroom, eating, or drinking anything. I was so totally focused on what was in front of me that I lost track of everything else around or inside of me. My senses of time and self disappeared, and I was only producing the task I was faced with. I often came home with a headache from hunger and dehydration, so she started setting herself an alarm so she could call me in the middle of the day and remind me to eat. It helped, but it also took me a few minutes to get back into the flow after eating. I can do the same in a CrossFit workout now and while public speaking.

Athletes often describe their best performances as having been the most effortless. The foundation for doing difficult things excellently and seemingly effortlessly is a combination of frequency and capacity. You have to have done difficult things over and over again so many times that your brain can reproduce the results without engaging too much awareness. It's second nature. Instinct. It also needs to be that the things that you have done over and over again are of sufficient difficulty to produce the required capacity for performance. An athlete can only do in a flow state what is comprised of foundational movements that he or she has already done in practice thousands of times and can, therefore, do without thinking.

One way to recharge your batteries is to do things that you can do in a flow state. This is a state of paradox, where you can be highly productive and rest the awareness centers of the brain at the same time. A flawless dance performance, a day of creative writing, or a perfect game of sports is the realm of high-capacity performers, and it's not much different than meditation from a psychological standpoint. It's a high-functioning state of rest.

Steven Kotler has done a lot of research on flow (Kotler, 2014). He notes that your brain begins to utilize less of the prefrontal cortex in a state of flow. That's where your awareness of time is, so your sense of time gets lost. It's also where you hold most of your anxieties since these are generally tied to time in the sense that they are traumas that happened in the past or concerns about what may happen in the future. Most of our anxieties aren't in the present, so when we lose track of past and future, we also lose track of our anxieties. Win-win.

This helps us to be freer and more creative. We're not trapped in time, and we're not living in fear. So we're much more creative, and our brains reward us by releasing a bunch of fun chemicals, including dopamine, serotonin, norepinephrine, anandamide, and endorphins. All of these chemicals have positive impacts on performance, both physically and neurologically. We're literally stronger, faster, and smarter. Also, they're addictive. Flow is addictive.

When you first learn to do something, the learning takes place in the frontal lobes of the brain. Like when you first learned to drive a car or read in a new language, it takes a lot of awareness and a lot of brain power because it's new. But over time, the brain builds neural networks for dealing with repetitive patterns to make your processing more efficient. It takes things that you do over and over again and moves them into the subconscious areas of the brain, things like brushing your teeth, or swinging a golf club, or reading a financial statement. After a while, you can do things without thinking about them consciously because you've done them over and over again, even things that seem complex to most people.

You can also learn new things in a flow state if they are in an area in which you already have some experience or expertise. In a great Mindvalley talk, Kotler claims that the neurochemical bath of flow increases learning by 470 percent, and research is showing that the 10,000 hours that Malcolm Gladwell says are needed for mastery of anything is effectively cut in half by learning in a flow state (Mindvalley, 2019).

The godfather of flow psychology is Mihaly Csikszentmihalyi (1990), who describes the state of flow as having eight characteristics:

1. Complete concentration on the task
2. Clarity of goals and reward in mind and immediate feedback
3. Transformation of time (speeding up/slowing down)
4. The experience is intrinsically rewarding
5. Effortlessness and ease
6. A balance between challenge and skills
7. Actions and awareness are merged, losing self-conscious rumination
8. A feeling of control over the task (Oppland, 2019)

But knowing what the state is like and getting there are two different things. We need to be able to make choices and pursue disciplines that can produce the flow state. Csikszentmihalyi and

Kotler have identified ten triggers that help to get us into a flow state:

1. Passion/purpose: doing something meaningful to you
2. Risk: the marginal possibility of failure
3. Novelty: something interesting and exciting to you
4. Complexity: something that requires complex ideas and thought
5. Unpredictability: involving a changing environment or set of rules
6. Deep embodiment: being deeply present, in the moment
7. Immediate feedback: something that gives you a sense of doing well/poorly while you are doing it
8. Clear goals: you know why you are doing it
9. Challenge-skills ratio: the challenge of the task at hand stretches our skills to the utmost
10. Creativity/pattern recognition: it's something that we've done before, and the activities required are rehearsed (Kotler, 2018; Mindvalley, 2019)

The key to getting into the flow state isn't just the environment you're in but your focus, combined with the thousands of repetitions that happened before that flow state, which allows your brain to build automated brain-body responses to information. This is why I can write and rest at the same time. I've simply done tens of thousands of hours of it, and the environment almost doesn't matter anymore. I wrote a lot of my best research in cafés, surrounded by noise. No matter how much attention you put into creating the right environment for yourself, you can only really flow in activities that are automated for you by a sufficient number of repetitions as to make their components largely instinctual.

Spartans know that they will perform at their best when they are doing what needs to be done in a flow state, so they build up the thousands of repetitions required to create that state for specific behaviors. Only the discipline to repeat a learned behavior thousands of times earns you the right to rest while you do it.

The first repeatable behavior that people often use to enter the state of flow is breathing. Yes, you can focus on breathing and get into flow (meditation). Some suggest that meditation is a prerequisite for flow. I don't agree since I can get into flow without it, but I can understand why so many would think so. The discipline of meditation slows your thoughts down, relieves distractions, controls breathing, and helps to pull your brain into that 8 Hz brainwave border where flow lives. Meditation is flow without an activity, and flow is meditation with an activity.

Mindfulness

Meditation is a broad umbrella term for practicing the ability to control what goes on in the mind and body. There are dozens, if not hundreds, of kinds of meditation, one of which is called mindfulness. Mindfulness as a subset of meditation is the practice of awareness mastery. Since mindfulness is controlled awareness, it's useful as a precursor to a flow state. But controlled awareness is especially difficult these days, with digital distractions every 40 seconds linked to neurochemical opioid rewards for being distracted. One study shows that we are typically mentally disengaged for around 47 percent of the workday (Killingsworth & Gilbert, 2010), and just as focus and flow lead to happiness, so does distraction lead to unhappiness. So Spartans develop the mental toughness for focus and awareness by using mindfulness.

To get started, think about what you are doing now. How mindful are you right now? Let's check. Become aware of your neck. Does it hurt? Is it in a good position? What about your feet? Are they warm, cool, in pain? Now your heart rate. Is it relaxed, accelerated? Is your awareness of your heartrate causing it to accelerate or decelerate? And your breathing: through your nose, mouth, or both? Slow or fast? Shallow or deep? Now be aware of your hearing. How many different sources of sound can you hear? Count them. Now your eyes. What do you see? Without changing what you are looking at, try to identify objects in your peripheral view. What can you see that you had not been aware of?

Now choose: Choose to feel relaxed. Choose to breathe slower. Choose to lower your heart rate by calming your mind, relaxing your muscles, and focusing on one present thing such as your breathing. Tune out all of what you hear until you only hear your own breath. Choose to focus your thoughts on only your breathing. Stay there. When your mind shifts to other things, gently bring it back to your breathing. Do this for 10 minutes.

One study of 239 employees has found that those who regularly practiced mindfulness or yoga were less stressed and slept better than those who didn't (Wolever et al., 2012). This backs up an earlier foundational study showing that mindfulness not only reduces stress but improves the immune system (Davidson et al., 2003).

So after including mindfulness among your disciplines, you are likely to notice some of these documented benefits:

1. An increase in productivity and creativity
2. A decrease in knee-jerk behavior that is often linked to poor decision making and damaging relationships
3. An increase in the density of gray matter in the brain area essential for focus, memory, and compassion
4. A decrease in blood pressure, cortisol (the stress-related hormone), and depression
5. An increase in immune response, emotional stability, sleep quality, and resilience and some offset of age-related cognitive decline (Gibson, 2019)

That's mindfulness in a nutshell: the ability to be aware and to control your awareness. It's tougher than it sounds and much more powerful. The focus that you have on your breathing that leads to a state of relaxation you can use on any activity that you've done a thousand times and achieve the same state.

Now, what do you do for more than half of your life every day that you can learn to do in a happy and relaxed, high-performing state? Work. Yes, your job. A lot of what you do at work you can do in flow by using mindfulness to get there. You'll be happier and healthier and make fewer mistakes.

We make bad decisions when we're stressed, and mindfulness pulls us into a relaxed state so that we can see things with fewer biases and heuristics in the way of noticing the opportunities in front of us. One study showed this effect specifically benefiting entrepreneurs, exposing and allowing them to think outside of a sunk cost bias that they had been stuck in (Hafenbrack, Kinias, & Barsade, 2014). We're able to measure the specifics of biases that are released during only 15 minutes of mindfulness. So what other biases could the executives of our large corporate communities be freed from if they were to choose the same discipline?

Mindfulness leads to less stress, better sleep, a stronger immune system, easy transition into flow at work, and fewer cognitive biases. These all have significant impacts on your decision-making quality and performance, and they can significantly affect the bottom-line performance of any organization run by humans. What difference do you think this will make in your life or to your quality of work if you practice mindfulness? And what difference will it make on the bottom line of a company whose executives regularly practice mindfulness compared to those whose don't?

We have all met those managers who seem to accomplish more in less time and with less struggle than their colleagues. Now you know their secret weapons. But do you have the focus and discipline to wield them?

Organizational Rest and Flow
The Cornell study above gives us a model for predicting and measuring productivity losses based on the sleeping patterns of our employees. If our people aren't resting enough, the owners of the company will ultimately pay for it. Measurements of keystroke and click timings show that people who slept more than six hours

for two consecutive nights performed 7.3 percent better than the average. Those who slept less than six hours for two nights in a row performed 4.8 percent slower than the average, with the negative effects lasting six days (Althoff et al., 2017).

So here's the math: a weekend warrior who parties really hard for two nights before coming into work will perform 12.1 percent lower than he or she would if he or she had slept well over the weekend. The impact will remain throughout the week. So if that person's salary is, say, $3,000/monthly, that's a productivity loss of roughly $90 to the company. Now, say you have a thousand employees who party hard. What then? That's why some companies have added sleep pods or napping rooms to help their people catch up and to minimize the cost of sleeplessness to the company.

Even worse, let's say an executive with a USD $500K salary struggles to sleep more than six hours a night over the weekend. That's a realized cost of $1,260 that the company pays for every low-sleep weekend. Now, let's say that it's chronic. For example, the executive is an insomniac, or a workaholic, or is trying to prove him- or herself by working until midnight every night. You can wipe $60,000 off of the net profit line from this year for that one executive's performance losses only due to sleep deprivation, and this doesn't account for increases in poor decision making or missed opportunity costs, only for the slower pace of action. Am I getting your attention? Anyone in the C-suite should be given a bonus for wearing a sleep monitor and protecting their seven-hour-a-night average.

So now that we know how much employees should sleep, we need to discuss how much they work. We know that work and life are blended now, not balanced, but we need some way of articulating how much work is counterproductive. Spoiler alert: the number is 40 hours per week.

Most companies were driving their people insane with 80-hour workweeks up to the mid-nineteenth century. Eventually, the workers unionized and pushed back, forcing the 10-hour limited workday in the United States and the United Kingdom. Not only did the owners of those companies accept it, but it began to become standard practice as more and more companies realized greater profitability with the 50-hour week than they had ever had before. In 1914, Henry Ford followed the logic and created the 40-hour week, which became the national standard in the New Deal in 1937. From then on, the 40-hour workweek was an institutionalized and largely unquestioned best practice.

Then the '80s and '90s hit, and cost-cutting measures were carried out with massive layoffs, which meant that there were fewer people to do more work. Sixty- to 80-hour workweeks became "normal" again for a while, especially in higher management, where naked apes in fancy suits were struggling to prove their value to boards of directors and their ax-wielding corporate consultants. It was assumed again, in spite of a century and a half of evidence to the contrary, that more hours equal more productivity. Ah, the lies we tell ourselves to look important. Humans can be pretty stupid sometimes.

Working longer hours leads to reduced productivity, poorer performance, and more costly mistakes (Robinson, 2012). Even during an overtime sprint, as a rule of thumb, management should expect the productivity gain to be around half a percent for every percent of overtime. So if the company is paying time and a half of salary for overtime, this means that for every hour of overtime (+12.5 percent increase in time), at 150 percent of the hourly rate, and at half the rate of productivity due to fatigue, the cost of the overtime hour on the final balance sheet is in fact 300 percent of the standard rate of pay.

Didn't follow? Jack is paid $10 an hour. He is working overtime today. The overtime hour costs the company $15, but Jack is tired, and the research shows that he'll only be about 50 percent productive during the extra hour, which means that the actual cost of a normal productive hour to the company (two overtime hours) is $30 an hour, not $15 and definitely not $10.

Not resting is expensive for everyone. Spartans know this. We don't get up at 5:00 a.m. unless we're in bed by 10:00 p.m. the previous night. We don't work unproductive hours. And when we're productive, we accelerate that productivity by doing as much as we can in a flow state. So what this means from an organizational perspective is that you Spartan leaders should be requiring your managers to rest, take time off, meditate, and limit their hours and those of their teams, and whenever possible at work, you should be encouraging flow states.

Yes, flow can be achieved on a team. University of North Carolina psychologist Keith Sawyer extended the triggers list above by identifying ten triggers that produce "group flow" (Sawyer, 2017):

1. Shared goals (everyone in the group is working toward the same end)

2. Close listening (you're paying complete attention to what is being said)
3. "Yes, and …" (conversations are additive, not combative)
4. Complete concentration (total focus in the right here, right now)
5. A sense of control (each member of the group feels in control but still flexible)
6. Blending egos (each person can submerge his or her ego needs into the group's)
7. Equal participation (skill levels are roughly equal, and everyone is involved)
8. Familiarity (people know one another and understand their tics and tendencies)
9. Constant communication (a group version of immediate feedback)
10. Shared, group risk (everyone has some skin in the game) (Kotler, 2018)

Flow is commonly preceded by mindfulness, remember? This is a practice gaining traction in the Fortune 500 firms. General Mills, Apple, Google, and Nike have all embraced the profitability of mindfulness as it improves organizational culture and learning performance (Cacioppe, 2017). Aetna Insurance's experience with mindfulness is a great case study (Gelles, 2016) highlighting the corporate benefits of mindfulness programming. Gelles notes that:

1. A highly stressed employee costs the company an extra $2,000 per year in healthcare when compared to less-stressed peers.

2. Healthcare costs at Aetna, which total more than $90 mil-
   lion a year, are going down now that they offer mindfulness programs.
3. In 2012, as mindfulness programs ramped up, healthcare costs fell a total of 7 percent. (That equals $6.3 mil-
   lion going straight to the bottom line, partly attributed to
   mindfulness training.)
4. Aetna calculated that productivity gains alone were
   about $3,000 per employee, equaling an 11-to-1 return
   on investment (Levin, 2017).

That's an amazing cost savings and net profit benefit realized in
a short period of time. The fact is all employees are humans (not
resources), and the more we understand the science of better
human performance and align our organizations to making sure
that our humans have every opportunity to perform better, the
better they will perform and the better we will all do as a corporate community.

For organizations that want to introduce a mindfulness program
but don't know where to start, I like Chris Altzier's list of principles for HR managers to consider. I'll give them to you as he
wrote them since I couldn't have paraphrased them any better
myself:

1. Make clear the company's intention behind introducing
   mindfulness in the workplace, focusing on performance
   and wellness as well as cost and productivity;
2. For employee wellness, include mindfulness training as
   a part of the basket of wellness options provided in the

workplace; provide training in a basic set of yoga poses and breathing practices suitable for the desk as well as in class;

3. For teams, if you have a template of team-start practices such as chartering, goal setting, or norm development, include a mindfulness practices overview and process to accelerate familiarity;

4. For leaders, if you have a leadership development curriculum, include mindfulness training for self-management and the challenges of leading;

5. Communicate well enough that the adoption of mindfulness practices, breathing exercises, yoga power poses, and meditation is not unexpected at the desk or meeting room;

6. Do not make participation or practice mandatory, and allow the practices to happen in the workplace while maintaining nonreligious standards;

7. Integrate mindfulness with your other workplace wellness strategies, including personal and workplace fitness and nutrition; and

8. Get professional advice; just as you engage reputable professionals for employee services, team consulting, or leadership development, engage certified professionals to inform the introduction and provision of mindfulness practices in the workplace. (Altizer, 2017)

A note on #3: If you don't know what a mindfulness practices process is, it's a plan to use mindfulness intentionally in the team-formation and operations processes. For example, a newly formed team can make excellent use of its time by conducting a breathing exercise for only 10 minutes before starting a weekly debriefing meeting. It will lower anxiety, clarify thoughts, and make the rest of the time in the meeting more fruitful and less emotional or individualistic in nature. This decreases the time required to settle challenges or differences during the meeting and makes the collective decision-making process more collaborative and effective, thereby compensating for the 10-minute investment of time in the beginning.

It's also important to promote mindfulness, especially at the top levels. Keep in mind that leader mindfulness has a measurable impact on improving employee performance and reducing employee stress. Recent science is revealing that not only do mindful leaders perform better, but some of the benefits of mindfulness trickle down the organizational chart (Schuh, Zheng, Xin, & Fernandez, 2019).

Breathe in.
Breathe out.
You've got this.

Spartan Core Finisher

1. Working long hours and sleeping less is absolutely nothing to brag about. The next time someone brags about only getting four to five hours of sleep a night because they're working 18-hour days, fire them. They're useless, and they don't know how to manage themselves.
2. Sleep more than seven hours a night, no nights off.
3. You can train no days off but not if you're pushing for max reps. Your body needs enough time to heal, and most

training pain can be dealt with in about 24 to 48 hours with proper rest.

4. Learn to practice mindfulness. The cognitive benefits are massive, and it's a best practice of high-performing leaders for a reason.

5. Whenever you can, avoid paying overtime. Put more people on the case instead. You'll get normal productivity and pay normal wages instead of 300 percent premiums on fatigued efforts. Too much work is not good for your people, and it's not good for your company.

6. Bring mindfulness and flow into the cultural language of your team, department, or organization. It's a low-cost, high-reward investment.

7. Try yoga.

Defining Moments

1. Your first yoga class
2. Your first 30-minute uninterrupted meditation
3. Leading a 10-minute mindfulness opener in a corporate meeting
4. Setting a policy for rest in your organization
5. Getting no less than seven hours of sleep a night for a whole month

Questions for Consideration

1. How much sleep are you getting every night? How much should you be getting? What decisions can you make to ensure you're at your best, no nights off?

2. Are you mindful? Can you concentrate in a state of focused awareness for a period of time? What can you do to improve your quality of thought by using mindfulness?
3. Are you encouraging your team members to rest? Be greedy enough to want them at their best. What changes can you make to encourage adequate rest in your organization?

Pillar 6

You Become as Fit as Your Frenemies

MiniSpartan Workout
This is a partner workout, so you'll need to enlist someone to complete this with you.

2 rounds for time of:

- 30 synchro kettlebell deadlifts at 16 kg / 35 lb. for men, 12 kg / 25 lb. for women (you both lift at the same time, so you need 2 kettlebells for this)
- 20 synchro sit-ups (synchro means "at the same time")
- 10 over-the-bar synchro burpees (do your burpees at the same time and then jump over the bar at the same time)
- Wallball run, 6 kg / 13 lb. for men, 4 kg / 9 lb. for women, 400 m (One of you carries the ball; the other runs beside. Share the load by passing the ball back and forth as necessary.)

Spartan Workout
This is a partner workout, so you'll need to enlist someone to complete this with you.

3 rounds for time of:

- 40 deadlifts at 100 kg / 220 lb. for men, 70 kg / 175 lb. for women (one lifts, one rests—split up the reps between you)
- 30 synchro sit-ups (both of you do 30 at the same time, same pace)
- 20 synchro bar-facing burpees (both do your burpees at the same time and then jump over the bar at the same time)
- Wallball run, 12 kg / 25 lb. for men, 9 kg / 20 lb. for women, 400 m (One of you carries the ball; the other runs beside. Share the load by passing the ball back and forth as necessary.)

This is another great partner workout, but this time, I want you to pay attention to your strengths and weaknesses in comparison to your partner. Are they faster than you at certain activities? Are you stronger than them in others? For added benefit, find another couple and make a race out of it. Two teams of two competing to see which pair can finish this workout first. Notice how adding the race element pushes all four of you to perform better.

Son of Zeus

I couldn't believe it. There was that prick's name on the top of the whiteboard again. I wouldn't have minded so much, but his lead over me was immense nearly every day. We would do a 15-minute AMRAP in CrossFit, and I would finish 6 rounds, while he would do eight. Or we would do a workout for time, and I would finish in 12 minutes, but he would finish in nine. He was fast, really fast, and I was always chasing him, but I had no idea who he was. I just knew that if I worked harder, I'd get my name up there one day, at the top of the whiteboard, ahead of fucking Toby!

I did get faster. I gained on him and closed the gap between us, but it was a long time before I beat him. One day, it finally happened. It was deadlift day. I'm good at deadlifts, and I was near my personal record at that time, so I could lift heavy consistently. And that was my angle. That was the missing link in Toby's armor. It was a max-3 set, and I did 190 kg (420 lb.) and took my place at the top, well ahead of him. I gave myself a mental fist-bump and walked away proud. It happened again, on another deadlift day. I crushed it. And again. I couldn't beat this guy in anything except deadlifts, and that became my signature. We eventually met up in class and competed with each other directly sometimes. I chased him down as well as I could but could never quite catch him in anything except that one lift.

Months went by before I finally figured out why. At our gym, on someone's birthday, the whole CrossFit class does birthday burpees, the same number as the birthday person is old. So we did birthday burpees for Toby on his birthday, all 28 of them! What the actual fuck? He was 15 years younger than I was.

Well. Huh.

Now, to be fair, Toby was in amazing shape. We called him the Son of Zeus for good reason. His power-to-weight ratio was better than anyone's I'd ever worked out with before. He was really fast and had amazing endurance. We both started running obstacle course races at about the same time, and though I could never catch up to him, I would always use him as a benchmark for my own performance. He trained more than I did, too, and took his athletics and diet more seriously. Plus, he was 28 (facepalm). I was never going to catch Toby, but training with him, and against him, made me better.

I told him this story one time. I think we were at a party together or something. I told him I was chasing him down for several weeks before we met. He told me that it irritated him to see my name at the top from time to time.

"Who the fuck is Corrie?" he said.

No one. Just a friendly competitor … 15 years his senior.

Haha.

#fucktoby

(Dear Toby, you'll never know how strong I got chasing you down and never catching you. Thank you for that.)

Mike

That reminds me of another time I kept getting my ass handed to me in a sport. I was in high school and couldn't beat my friend Mike in badminton to save my life. It was grade 11, and after school, we would hit the 7–11 for a Slurpee and a Mars chocolate bar and then head to his place to watch Darkwing

Duck and eat a box of Kraft Mac-n-Cheese before I walked home for dinner. It was a really unhealthy diet plan, but I survived it.

Anyway, when the weather was good, we went outside to play badminton in his yard. He taught me how to play, and I got better, but I could never seem to beat him. It took weeks before I scored a point at all and months before I could finish the game with several points. I didn't get tired of losing because I knew I was always getting better. I would lose with more points earned and found my solace in those marginal gains.

Then I traveled for the summer, and while on vacation, I had the opportunity to play badminton with a few people who had some experience. It was really fun. I crushed them without too much effort too. I couldn't believe it.

When I got back home, I went over to Mike's place again to play a game. I told him about how I crushed it in a few friendly games and thanked him for his training. That was the time he picked to tell me that he had been on the podium at the Provincial badminton tournaments in earlier years. I suppose he could have told me sooner, but where would the fun have been in that? Plus, I might not have agreed to play if I had known he was really good.

#fuckmike

(Dear Mike, thank you for being so patient with a rookie like me. Let's go curling sometime.)

My point is that these are two times in my life when I was training with people who were better than I was, and I became better for it. Very few people are the best in the world at something. For the rest of us, there are two dominant strategies for becoming amazing at something: strong competition and strong coaching. Either will help. Both are better.

Thomas
I did my first doctoral degree at Exeter University in the United Kingdom. It was exhilarating. I spent thousands of hours in my tiny below-ground office in my home studying. Since I was already adept at dropping into a flow state for research, I could sit myself down on my chair and within minutes be reading at supersonic speeds, engaged in deep thought, and often I wouldn't be aware of my surroundings again until the wee hours of the morning. I recall a few times being jolted back to reality by the sound of my family waking up to get ready for school.

My first wife often remarked that I spent too much time in my own head and encouraged me to "get out of your head more often and see what's going on around you." When I traveled to Exeter to meet my supervisor, I traveled alone. I sat from morning to night in the library, alone. I wrote and rewrote, carved out my tiny kingdom of thought leadership, and defended it, alone. Or at least that's what it would have looked like to an outsider.

In truth, I was never alone. I was just deeply engaged with people who weren't with me. I had daily philosophical debates with authors who had been dead for a thousand years or more. As I was studying history, many of my sources were written by people who had passed away centuries, and sometimes a millennium, ago. But they were alive in my mind. They had voices, ideas, contexts, and emotions all playing out in my mind, and the space in my head where I studied the historical debates on which I wrote my thesis was, in fact, a crowded room filled with giants on whose shoulders I dared to stand.

Many of my closest friends at that time had been deceased for ages, and yet they were very alive to me. Their passions and concerns were salient and emotive. When they had been separated from each other by centuries of time, and thousands of kilometers, I took it upon myself to give them some space in my head where, based on my limited interaction with their legacies of written works, they could speak to one another, debate each other, and perhaps even find common ground that they might have missed when they were living. I was in the company of the thought leaders of their ages, all crammed together in an imaginary majlis. It was thrilling, and I felt more like a facilitator of a long-overdue conversation than a reader of history. I was humbled and proud to be in the company of powerful thinkers whose ideas had stretched out past the Crusades, through the Middle Ages, surviving the burning of the library of Baghdad, enduring the rises and falls of empires, the Enlightenment, the Industrial Revolution, and the World Wars.

It is every historian's responsibility to remove him- or herself from the conversation and yet every historian's privilege to listen in and faithfully steward the events as objectively as possible just the same. It was in those imagined spaces that I became my strongest. I hit my mental and psychological personal records; I

leaped over philosophical walls, dodged flaming arrows of judgment, assumption, bias, presupposition, and gained the Olympic
skill of holding mutually exclusive "truths" together without suc-
cumbing to the fatigue of paradox or the temptation of forced
resolution. I was at my strongest because I was training along-
side the strongest in my field. No. Days. Off.

The time from acceptance of my PhD proposal to my *viva voce*
was 21 months. In that time, I consumed more than 1,000 books
and journal articles, ultimately producing the finest mental performance of my career to that point. I could not have done it without
my coach, Dr. Ian Richard Netton, and my training compatriots, a
bibliography of hundreds of authors. I also had a cheering section
comprised of my family, neighbors, and friends, who often stared
at me with compassionate curiosity when I tried to expound on
my most recent learning.

For any who have completed a PhD, you know that training with
the best is only preparatory work for the final test, the defense.
Mine was a defining moment since I was to be examined by Dr.
David Thomas. It was my Blackbelt exam.

I stepped into the room to face my examiners alone, without my
coach by my side and no cheering section. Across the table sat
Dr. Thomas, whose name and materials had made more than a
dozen appearances in my own work. He was the living master of
our trade to whom I would have to demonstrate the skills I had
learned from training with the hundreds of thought warriors I had
worked with over the preceding months. He was the best in the
world in our field, fully competent in the concepts and periods I
had studied, and I was terrified.

The examiners grilled me on my sources, materials, lines of reasoning, and, most dangerously, my conclusions. About three hours into the ordeal, something strange happened: Dr. Thomas and I had sparred quite naturally into a third debate in which we held opposing views. I dropped into a flow state for the remainder of the discussion. I let go of my fears, my awareness of the environment disappeared, and my sense of time slipped away. For every challenge he brought, I had a ready and eloquent response, and I remember the first time I had the thought, *I think I might know more about this than he does.* I kept it to myself, but it was a defining moment for me when I became the teacher. I was able to introduce a fresh perspective on materials we were both familiar with, and my examiner, clearly as skilled and as comfortable as I was at holding unresolved paradoxes in mind, accepted my argument. There was no need to win; the competition was enough for him to know that he was now in the room with a colleague, no longer a student.

I felt it happen, like a surfer dropping into a 50-foot wave, fully confident in my command of a potentially crushing experience. Thousands of hours of reading came back to me. I had instant access to all that I had learned, and I could hear the voices of the interlocutors in my head feeding me the ideas that they had scrawled onto parchment a dozen lifetimes ago. It was exhilarating, effortless, and dynamic. I was martensite: shape-shifting metal, fluid and strong. I never knew what was coming next, but somehow I knew I would be able to handle it, whatever it was.

Then, suddenly, Dr. Thomas stood up, reached out his hand, and said, "Congratulations, Doctor." I was torn out of my flow state and immediately became aware of the room again. I felt my thirst for the first time. I remember a twinge of disappointment that this incredibly high-quality conversation was over. I wanted it to keep going. Aside from my coach, I hadn't had any living person challenge me so expertly on my training since I had started the process. I didn't want the exam to end.

It was over in four hours. Approved. Straight to publication. I knew right then that if I could do that in only 21 months of hard-core training in a field as foreign and esoteric as Arab history, I could do it again—in any field of my choosing. I wasn't just a historian; I was a world-class athlete in thought leadership, and I had earned my place on the leaderboard in a narrow field of pin-nacle thinkers spanning more than a thousand years.

My coach, Dr. Netton, was pleased with the news but not sur-prised. He knew I was capable of more than I thought myself capable of. He knew the endless hours in the basement would pay off in the exam. He had seen and approved my work before the test had begun, and he believed in me.

I had trained with the best, sparred with the best, and earned the right to count myself among them. After all, you can only become as fit as those you train with.

#fuckthomas

(Dear Dr. Thomas, thank you for one of the best conversations of my life and for a defining moment that I'll never forget.)

You're as Fit as Your Friends

Okay, so it appears that there's no significantly scientific finding to support your mother's warning that you are the sum of
your seven closest friends. However, that doesn't mean that your
social networks have no influence on you at all. Christakis and
Fowler (2007) have discovered over a 32-year study of 12,000
people that some behaviors are socially contagious. If your sibling is obese, you're only 40 percent more likely to be obese yourself, but if you have a friend who becomes obese, your chances
of becoming obese go up by 57 percent, and you can't blame
genetics for that. Among spouses, it's 37 percent. Same-sex
relationships were more influential than opposite-sex relationships in this study.

But peer pressure works in good ways too. If your spouse quits
smoking, you're 67 percent more likely to quit too. If your sibling
quits, it's only 25 percent more likely that you will, but if your
friend quits, you're 36 percent more likely to quit too. And that
number is pretty consistent for coworkers. If your coworker quits
smoking, you're 34 percent more likely to quit yourself. In the
smoking study, relationships between more highly educated
people were more influential than relationships between less
educated people (Christakis & Fowler, 2008).

So what can we learn from this? Obesity is socially contagious,
but so is quitting smoking. Oh, and friends are more influential,
both positively and negatively, than siblings. So water is thicker
than blood in terms of social behavioral influence, and one of
the most powerful influences is a spouse. Remember when I
told you that I first started exercising alone, and after three
weeks my first wife decided to join in the fun? I didn't tell her to

go to the gym. I didn't pressure her at all. I just went, every day, no days off. She saw what was happening to me and decided to align herself with my new behavior. So, no, I don't recommend going home and telling your wife that she needs to hit the gym and lose that last bit of arm flab. Not cool. Instead, an effective methodology is to hit the gym yourself and see if it catches on.

If you're having trouble getting motivated to make a change in your life, you can hack yourself by hanging out with people who have already made that change. Wanna start a business? Make friends with entrepreneurs. Wanna write a book? Go hang out at an authors' meetup. Wanna start taking illegal drugs? Hang out with people who take drugs. You get the point. If your friends do it, positively or negatively, your chances of aligning your behavior to theirs go up significantly. As it turns out, your mom was right when she warned you that "peer pressure is a real thing, y'know."

The same researchers took another 20-year dataset and found out that happiness is contagious too. Perhaps it's no surprise that if you are surrounded by happy people, you are more likely to be happy yourself, but consider this: if a friend of a friend of your friend is happy, then you have a 6 percent better chance of being happy too (Fowler & Christakis, 2008). Happiness is contagious even at social distances. So all of the mind hacks you've learned for improving your and others' happiness in the preceding chapters, that's all going to have a viral effect in the social circles that you're connected to.

We know that we tend to reflect and repeat the behaviors of those closest to us. This can be both a bad thing and a good thing. If you're intentional about who you spend your time with and connect with, you can gather the kinds of friends around you who will naturally pull you in the direction of positive change. Being included in a group is a powerful performance influence, especially when the group can choose its membership and reward its members.

You're as Fit as Your Workgroup

A study by Stewart, Courtright, and Barrick (2012) has found that teams tend to perform better under both peer-based rational and normative control, with normative control being the stronger influence.

Wait! Don't run away. I'll translate that for those of you who aren't social scientists.

Normative control is when members of a group are motivated to behave a certain way because they feel a sense of connection or belonging to the group. For example, Greg works well in the group because he feels like he's a part of the group. Rational control is when members of a group are motivated to behave a certain way because of individual desires to achieve carrots and avoid sticks. For example, Greg works well in the group because he knows that if the group doesn't do well, then he won't get the promotion he's aiming for. The study found that when people felt that either their belonging to the group or their rewards for performance were influenced by the group members themselves, they performed better. Interestingly, the rewards for performance became less important to individuals on the team as their sense of belonging increased.

So let's say you've charged an agile team of eight staff members with a group project for your department. What the research shows is that the members of the group will perform better if they each get a say in who gets to be in the group. That is, Greg will do better in a group where he feels like he gets a say in who gets to be a part of the group and where he feels that the other members of the group get a say in him being there.

Greg will also perform better if he feels that the other members of the group will get a say in his performance-based rewards—that is, in whether or not he will get the promotion he's aiming for. However, the influence of peer-based performance rewards goes down for members who feel that their sense of belonging to the group is going up. That's a good thing. It means that if Greg feels like he's a valuable member of the group, he will be less motivated by his team's influence on his potential promotion and more influenced by his sense of belonging. In other words, people who belong more perform better. Inclusion has a direct positive impact on group performance.

So let's review: If you want to make a change in your life, you can surround yourself with people who are making that change. The fact that you are included and they have the opportunity to kick you out of the group will make it even more likely that you will perform well. Also, if you know that you will be rewarded by the group for good performance, like by getting an Instagram "like" from them for posting your in-group goal achievement, your performance will go up even more.

Business Is Football, Not Basketball

In the *My Little Hundred Million* episode of Malcolm Gladwell's Revisionist History podcast (2017), Gladwell makes a wonderful presentation of the differences between football and basketball in terms of team development. Football, says Gladwell, is a weak-link sport. Since it takes a number of ball passes to get the ball up the field and into a position where a star player can score, the weak links are where development should happen. Team owners can accomplish a lot more by investing in upgrading the average player rather than upgrading the one or two star players since no star player can run the field and score with any consistency.

It's not the same for basketball teams. Basketball is a strong-link sport. In basketball, one star player can run the length of the court, towering over the opposition and charging through defenses without assistance. The dominant strategy in basketball is to not invest in your weakest players but to upgrade the one or two stars who can run the court alone and score consistently.

Business is football, not basketball. Star players are interesting from a marketing perspective, but star players can't select raw materials; operate the manufacturing; provide quality assurance, logistics, and employee care; monitor KPIs; and close the deal all by themselves. There's a long field of play in business, requiring a lot of passes before the ball can get to a star player to close a deal. It's the dominant strategy of the firm, therefore, to invest in upgrading the average employee rather than invest in upgrading the star performers. The weakest link is the most important player because they are holding back the average performance of the organization. In business, you're not as strong as your strongest players; rather, you're as weak as your weakest team members.

It's the same with departments in a corporate system. It doesn't matter how all-star your sales team is if your weak link is quality control or research and development. Smart leaders invest in upgrading their weakest links in business to raise the performance of the product or service offering from end to end. We upgrade our weakest links because business is a football game, not a basketball game, and our rivals are waiting for us in the middle of the field.

You're as Fit as Your Frenemies

Some of the best moments in sports are when rivals meet. Many world records have been set during competition, like Usain Bolt's 9.58-second 100-m sprint in the 2009 Summer Olympics or Mitchie Brusco's Big Air 1260 at the X-Games a decade later. Whether between the strongest women, the fastest men, or the two most successful teams in the final game of a knockout championship, we love a good rivalry between top-tier performers. Why? Because that's when world records get smashed. That's when they're at their best. That's when we're at our best too.

Ronaldo started playing professional football in 2001 and Messi only two years later. In 2007, they placed second and third behind Kaka for the Ballon d'Or trophy. For the next decade, the two men passed the trophy back and forth between them, winning five times each. As of today, Ronaldo is leading in all-time scoring with 700 over Messi's 672, but Messi is leading with a .81 scoring ratio over Ronaldo's .72, which is still 0.7 points per game higher than the next highest currently active player, Robert Lewandowski (scoring ratio of 0.65).

Ronaldo and Messi have one of the greatest friendly rivalries the sporting world has ever seen. The two men, playing for teams on opposing sides of the world, only meet each other on the field an average of twice a year. Yet they have been pushing each other's limits for their entire careers. Ronaldo confirmed the frenemy thesis in an interview once, saying, "I have no doubt that Messi has made me a better player and vice versa. When I am winning trophies, it must sting him, and it's the same for me when he wins. We have an excellent professional relationship because we have been sharing the same moments for 15 years … We've never had dinner together, but I don't see why we can't in the future. I don't see a problem with that" (Sportstar, 2019). For a rival to be an effective performance influence on you, they don't have to be a nemesis.

Gavin Kilduff studied long-distance runners and found that runners ran a five-kilometer race a full 25 seconds faster when they had a rival in the race (Kilduff, 2014). But this is an old truth. The sixteenth-century rivalry between Raphael and Michelangelo drove both to produce art directly intended to best the other, and the resulting quality blankets the Sistine Chapel in Rome. The two outpainted each other so well that it drove the whole world of art forward by an epoch.

Competition like this is still driving innovation today. In 2004, Peter Diamandis awarded the Ansari Xprize of USD $10 million to Mojave Aerospace Ventures for SpaceShipOne. Virgin Atlantic licensed the technology, and the commercial space industry was born, from a deliberately fabricated competition. So what is it about competition, direct or indirect, that drives us to higher performance and innovation? And can we use that to redefine "competitive advantage" in business? What if competition itself *is* an advantage?

In the summer of 1997, one of the greatest business rivalries in history was coming to a grim end. Apple Computers Corporation was dying. With 90 days of cash flow left, the company scrambled for solutions. On July 9, Steve Jobs returned to Apple as interim CEO, and less than a month later, on August 6, he sold 150,000 shares of preferred convertible stock in Apple to then-rival Bill Gates of Microsoft for USD $150 million. Why would Microsoft do that? Why invest in propping up a competitor that way? Because competition drives innovation. Microsoft needed a rival as much as Apple needed the cash.

In a later interview, Jobs was asked why the deal was made and remarked, "There was just a lot of reasons for it that don't matter, but the net result of it was there were too many people at Apple, and in the Apple ecosystem, playing the game of 'for Apple to win, Microsoft has to lose.' And it was clear that you didn't have to play that game because Apple wasn't going to beat Microsoft. Apple didn't have to beat Microsoft. Apple had to remember who Apple was because they'd forgotten who Apple was" (Silver, 2018).

As Jobs highlighted, the Microsoft–Apple rivalry was a zero-sum game to many of the Apple employees. This meant that for Apple to win, Microsoft had to lose, and since Microsoft was clearly winning, Apple was clearly losing. Microsoft, rather, was playing an infinite game, and for a player to excel in an infinite game, competition is a necessity. Competition drives innovation. Microsoft didn't want to defeat Apple. In the same way that Messi and Ronaldo are in competitive symbiosis, Microsoft needed Apple in order for Microsoft to remain at its best. So Microsoft kept Apple in the game so it could have a rival to drive its own innovation.

Imagine if Messi was benched because somehow Barcelona couldn't pay him to play, and he was contracted not to play for any other team. Then imagine that Ronaldo offers to pay some of Messi's salary for a while to make sure he stays on the field. Why is this in Ronaldo's best interest? Ronaldo would do this just to make sure Messi plays because when Messi plays, Ronaldo is also at his best.

In 2001, Microsoft converted the last of its Apple shares to common stock and, in 2003, sold them and ended its investment in Apple. Microsoft only kept its competitor alive long enough for it to stand alone and run at a competitive speed again. Since then, it's been game on. The *TIME Magazine* cover in which the story was told famously features Steve Jobs crouched down on the phone next to his words in quote: "Bill, thank you. The world's a better place" (TIME, 1997).

And it is.

Can you imagine what might have happened if Bill had played the zero-sum game rather than the infinite game? The iMac, iPod, iPhone, Apple TV, Apple Music, and my favorite, Keynote—those Apple innovations disrupted major industries and have become some of the most influential tools on the planet. Plus, the continued rivalry led Microsoft to perform better in its Windows OS, enter the hardware game with the XBOX and the Surface products, and add a number of new fields on which the two giants have battled ever since. The constant battle has made them both stronger, and we mere consumers have all benefited from better tech at lower costs every year because of it.

Windows needed iOS, and the iPhone needs Samsung's Galaxy. And Samsung TVs need Sony's TVs, and on and on it goes. Great rivalries make players stronger than they can be on their own. So in case it's been a while since you've heard it, and you happen to be reading this book, "Bill, thank you again. The world really is a better place."

Find Your Toby

Toby, Mike, Dr. Thomas, thank you. I am fitter and smarter because I chose you all as rivals at some point and benchmarked my own growth against your performance, whether you knew it or not.

Reader, it's time to find your Toby. Identify someone who is able to do what you would like to do and compete with them. Whether you tell them or not doesn't matter so much, but if you and your frenemy are at about the same skill level, it will help you to develop a mutual rivalry. You will both be smarter, faster, stronger, more agile, better painters, more compelling dancers, more accurate golfers, funnier clowns. Whatever infinite game you are playing, identify a rival and use their performance to energize your own.

In a company, it's usually pretty easy to pick a rival; the problem is when we don't pick one aspirational enough. I was working on a marketing strategy for Seven Fortunes, a small coffee roastery in Dubai, a few years ago, and one of the exercises that my team went through was to identify the competitive landscape. Who are the local competitors, and against which of them should the small roastery benchmark itself? So we went through the marketing studies and available information and identified a number of boutique roasteries in the area. The best benchmark was another independent roastery called RAW Coffee Company. It would have been enough for us to list them off, along with their shares of the market, and lay out a plan to compete and conquer. But there was a problem. RAW wasn't Seven Fortunes' main competition.

The whole boutique roastery market was under threat. Not only were there a lot of players on the field fighting each other for market share, but the field was getting smaller and smaller. It was being eaten up by a macrotrend shifting home brewers away from coffee beans and bags of ground coffee to pods. Coffee pods, in the form of Nespresso and Dolce Vita mostly, were crushing the home-brewed coffee market in Dubai, replacing percolators and French presses like they were pagers and fax machines. What good would it be for me to tell my client to compete with RAW when both competitors were being disrupted by Nestle?

In the home coffee game, RAW and Seven Fortunes weren't competitors; they were allies in a larger game against Nestle. Both companies expanded in the direction of artisan brewing, adding Chemex, siphons, and cold brews to their list of offerings. This expanded the potential uniqueness of the home brew experiences too, allowing more opportunities for consumers to gear-head on their particular form of brewed coffee. They also both have coffee shops attached to their roasteries, which allow them to offer the café experience along with barista training for hardcore clients. In this way, they are allies, redefining coffee as a special, unique process with chemically fine-tuned variations catering to the individual palate. This is their collective opposition to Nestle's pods, which remove the brewing experience altogether as a convenience-based service offering.

In the artisanal café game, RAW and Seven Fortunes are competitors, but in home brew, they are allies in a larger game against Nestle. Starbucks is an artisanal café competitor, too, and look at how they've adapted to the disruption. Do you see shelves full of espresso makers in Starbucks anymore? Not so much. But you will find Starbucks branded pods, made specifically for the Nespresso machine, in nearly every Starbucks café and in most major grocery stores now. Starbucks had the coffee that people wanted, and Nestle had the delivery system that people were gravitating toward. It was only a matter of time before Nestle spent $7.1 billion in 2018 on the rights to package Starbucks coffee in Nespresso pods and sell them in grocery stores. How long will it be before RAW and Seven Fortunes are putting their artisanal coffee in Nespresso-fitting pods as well?

A game that Starbucks and Nespresso are unlikely to be able to compete in is the custom home brew game since convenience and mass production are antithetical to customization. In the custom home brew coffee game, RAW and Seven Fortunes would do well to keep promoting the value of having a unique-to-you brew. There, they will find the antiestablishmentarians as an expanding core of clients, holding back the pod-shaped tsunami, and each other, just as much frenemies as competitors.

When I'm out doing research and writing, like today, right now, you might find me at Seven Fortunes or RAW Coffee in Dubai. But at home, I'm a Nespresso client. Arpeggio, for those of you who care.

Community Competition

How can you apply all of this competitive innovation in your organization?

First, identify external frenemies. Which corporate communities are you competing with in what? Are you defining the game or following their rules? The wonderful thing about infinite games such as business is that the rules are constantly changing. Business is like football in the sense that the weakest players on your team will limit your team's competitiveness, but it's not like football in the sense that there is no start or end time, no agreed-upon rules, and the referees can decide which team gets points based on any personal preference they happen to have at the time.

One of the most ridiculous measures of success is the year-end annual report. The idea that the game ends on December 31 every year and starts up again the following year is just plain silly. But we still count up our points each year to see how we're doing and measure our points against our competitors'. The problem is that, more and more, successful competitors aren't paying attention to the points at all; they're paying attention to the referee.

The referee is your market. They're the ones who decide in which direction money should flow: To you? To your competitor? Or perhaps to another team on another field that just disrupted your game? I'm sure you understand how dangerously distracting the financial measures can be.

So it's not enough to just identify your competition; you must also identify disruptors that are eroding your field. You and your competitor are allies in that larger game. Yes, Mitchie Brusco stunned the world with his Big Air 1260 in the X-Games in 2019, but it was Elliot Sloan who took the gold medal in the event. Mitchie and Elliot, though competitors at the X-Games, are also allies in the larger world of competitive sports, drawing more and more viewers away from traditional sporting competitions to new and innovative ones.

Also, it's not enough to just identify your referee; you must also identify the rules of the game according to the referee's momentary preferences. The referees can change the rules at any time and award points to whomever they like. Yes, Seven Fortunes and RAW can compete with each other on barista training programs and special roasts of coffee to take home, but more and more consumers are moving points in the direction of convenience over customization. The Starbucks pods for Nespresso machines are a shift in the game that RAW and Seven Fortunes need to become allies in addressing, and the critical success factor is to unlock the referee's preferences, not to count points against Nestle and Starbucks.

Internally, you can leverage competition in your organization in the same way that Peter Diamandis did with the Ansari X-Prize. Identify a problem and have two or more teams work the same problem. They will likely approach the problem in different ways, and rather than choosing whether or not you like a particular solution, you will end up with more than one solution to choose from.

You can gamify the experience by enlisting a jury of representatives from various corporate departments and even include market representatives to deliberate on the solutions. Celebrate the distinctiveness of each outcome, award the winners, and set up a rematch with a new problem to be solved.

Conclusion

Whether personally or corporately, socially or professionally, you are limited by your choice of rival. A well-curated competition can help to produce amazing performance, even if it only exists in your own mind. Just be careful of the traps of competitiveness. One of the traps you can fall into is never being able to "win" against your chosen rival. If you are not clear that the ultimate goal of competition is self-improvement, then you can find the competitive exercise self-defeating. You might develop a narrative of ongoing defeat, and that can derail your growth.

Worse, you could fall into the other trap: obsession. Beating another person, team, or company can become the kind of obsession that robs you of your focus. You don't want to end up mentally in the same zero-sum game that Apple was in when they needed Microsoft's rescue in 1997. Again, maintain that even though you are competing at the moment, the goal of the competition isn't to win but to get better, faster, and stronger yourself and to look for new ways to play the game and maybe even new rules by which to play.

Spartan Core Finisher

1. You're only as fit as those you train with. Start surrounding yourself with people who have the skills and experience that you want to collect, and allow them to influence you. Peer pressure is a real thing, so put it to use in yourself and in those around you.
2. Sometimes your competitors in one game can be your allies in another game. Don't become hyperfocused on

any single player or you'll risk disruption from a player you didn't see coming.

3. Business is football, not basketball. Upgrade your weakest members in order to raise the average level of play on your team.

4. Respect your competition. Don't play the game to win, play the game to get better, faster, and stronger than you were yesterday. Your competitors are keeping you sharp.

Defining Moments

1. You identify a person in your industry that you will have a friendly competition with, whether they are aware of it or not.

2. You engage in a competition in which you or your organization were once the rookie, and you have now become the teacher.

3. You rescue a competitor from a zero-sum loss, so that you can continue to play a game with them that helps you to stay sharp.

4. You identify one of your competitors as an ally in a larger game.

Questions for Consideration

1. What are some of the things you would like to change in your life? Are the people surrounding you influencing you in that direction? Or do you need to add some new people to your life?

2. Who are your frenemies? Who are the people who have achieved something that you want to achieve in your field

of work? What intentional steps are you taking to remain competitive with them?

3. Are any of your competitors potential allies in a larger game?

4. Are you as sharp, fast, and strong as you should be in order to remain competitive in the coming decade of accelerating information? What changes do you need to make in order to get to your best, compete with the best, and break world records in your field?

Concluding Thoughts

I wrote this book as much to encourage myself to keep going as to share with you my best practices for a Spartan-style life. I try to be fit, not fat, but I'm not amazing at it. I'm a bit athletic, but I'm not a career athlete; I'm a consultant. I know who I am. I cracked my L3 vertebrae dropping into a concrete skate bowl in my early twenties, which has left me with a permanent impingement in my back. It makes squats very challenging and snatches nearly impossible. My shoulders are also chronically weak, and I need to be careful not to push them too far when I work out. I also drink beer and smoke sheesha on the weekends, which are things I could stop doing but choose not to. They remain a part of my definition of a high quality of life. I eat burgers and nachos and pizza and all of the bad things. I still go to the gym to earn the right to eat what I like, and I still like the bad things; that hasn't changed.

I enjoy going to the gym now, so that's good, but I'm still never going to be an Olympian. I work out because it's a part of my blended life. I eat well, and badly, depending on the day. I have regular exercise and days of laziness. I work really hard most days and other days not at all. I have a good blend of productive activities, and sometimes their opposing forces as well, in my life.

I've embraced both the limitations and the potential of my individual humanity: physically, mentally, and socially. I know who I am, and I want the same for you.

I do know that you can accomplish way more than you think you can. You are smarter, faster, stronger, and emotionally fitter than you give yourself credit for. Personally, when I look back on my first four decades of life, I am stunned by what I was able to accomplish. But it wasn't me accomplishing those things in a vacuum. I had people around me telling me that I was capable of more than I thought, and they were right.

I've started seven companies and failed at two of them. I've lost everything I had and dropped below the financial bankruptcy line three times in my life, and yet I've recovered each time. I've completed two masters and two doctorate degrees. I've had two brilliant kids and raised them with my ex-wife in Estonia during the days before supermarkets, in Yemen during the days before running water and electricity, and in Dubai during the difficult days leading up to our divorce. We even raised our kids during a year of civil war happening around us. I've been on the Al Qaeda hit list and escaped and buried two of my friends who were not as fortunate as I was. I've broken my back, survived Dengue fever, and driven the Taiz-Aden road back when it was one lane through the mountains. I built a sauna house in Estonia in −20°C weather, ran the Spartan Trifecta in two days, and fell off an iceberg into the Ottawa River and lived.

Each time, it was people around me, telling me that I was stronger than I thought I was, who convinced me I could do it. Taking on a challenge and surviving a crisis are similar projects, both requiring grit, and community has been my overwhelmingly primary critical success factor. Whether it was my teachers, family, friends, spouse, mentors, employees, or dead authors from long ago, I've always had voices surrounding me telling me that I was capable of more, much more, than I could have ever dreamed. Perhaps I'll write a book about those adventures someday too.

If you had asked me when I was young whether or not I was up to the challenge of living through all of those things, I would have likely opted out. But if you ask me now whether or not I would do it all again, the answer is yes. If given the option, I would do all of it again.

I am fitter because of it.

I learned discipline through it. I learned that even though I believed my friends and family that something was possible, I would still have to kick my own ass to get it done, whether finishing a degree, losing weight, or recovering from bankruptcy. I would have to choose behaviors that would lead to success, in spite of how I felt. I learned that motivation is weak and that success doesn't come from how I feel about something but from whether or not its completion would be meaningful to me and to those around me.

I learned to make eye contact and ask for help when I needed it. It led me to seek mentors, partners, and counselors along the way. I also learned to make eye contact when others were looking to me. Helping people is both rewarding and contagious. I valued it just as much when I could help someone else as I did when others helped me.

I learned to rest, to take time off, to truly unplug when necessary. I gave up on the workaholic's vice of frantic activity and focused my efforts on making more time more productive more often instead. I had no choice: there was a lot of work to do, and I was counting on me to do it. I dialed in my flow state so that I could do what came most naturally to me with wizardlike efficacy, not every day but most days and for more time each day than I used to do.

I learned who my competitors really were. They were my allies in a game that ultimately multiplied my own performance and productivity. Their presence on the planet was a gift to me when I felt tired, alone, or like I was facing an impossible task. They are my competitors because I choose them to be. I pick both them and the games we play together.

Now it's your turn. What is the job description of the Spartan CEO of your life?

First, stop being physically, mentally, emotionally, and spiritually unfit. Unless you have a diagnosed illness that prevents you from developing past your current state in any of those areas, acknowledge your laziness and get your ass in gear. What does Spartan-level self-leadership look like for someone in your circumstances? No more excuses; write it down.

Second, set clear and high goals for yourself. When people around you say that you are capable of more than you think, they're absolutely right, and you need to start believing them. They have your best interests at heart, and they aren't distracted by the voice in your head that says you can't do it.

Third, write down your disciplines. Turn your goals into small, replicable activities that you can do every day, week, or month and that will lead you to your definition of success. Then make the choice to do those things and hold yourself accountable. Spartan-level discipline is a matter of will—your will.

Fourth, help people and ask for help. Your life is a race that you cannot win alone, so be proactive about practicing and accepting community and helping behavior. Your work is a small piece of a community economic project. Get more involved in the communities of your life.

Fifth, get enough sleep. Take time off, and learn to do as much of your work as you can in a flow state. You'll be much happier and many times more productive if you rest well and work in flow. Spartans practice sleep and flow deliberately.

Last, choose good rivals and recognize them as allies in a game that will make you better yourself. Pushing against someone strong will make you both stronger. Be grateful for your frenemies and intentional about selecting them.

Spartan CEO, what is your profession?

Bibliography

Achor, S., Reece, A., Kellerman, G. R., & Robichaux, A. (2018). 9 out of 10 people are willing to earn less money to do more-meaningful work. *Harvard Business Review.* Retrieved from https://hbr.org/2018/11/9-out-of-10-people-are-willing-to-earn-less-money-to-do-more-meaningful-work.

Algoe, S. B., & Way, B. M. (2014). Evidence for a role of the oxytocin system, indexed by genetic variation in CD38, in the social bonding effects of expressed gratitude. *Social Cognitive and Affective Neuroscience* 9 (12), 1855–1861.

Althoff, T., Horvitz, E., White, R. W., & Zeitzer, J. (2017). Harnessing the web for population-scale physiological sensing: A case study of sleep and performance. Published in *Proceedings of WWW 2017.*

Altizer, C. (2017). Mindfulness: performance, wellness or fad? *Strategic HR Review* 16 (1), 24–31.

Amazon. (2019). *Leadership principles.* Retrieved from https://www.amazon.jobs/en/principles.

Bandura, A. (1997). *Self-efficacy: The exercise of control.* New York: W. H. Freeman.

Bar-Eli, M., Azar, O. H., Ritov, I., Keidar-Levin, Y., & Schein, G. (2007). Action bias among elite soccer goalkeepers: The case of penalty kicks. *Journal of Economic Psychology* 28, 606–621.

Baumeister, R., Brewer, L. E., Tice, D., & Twenge, J. M. (2007). Thwarting the need to belong: Understanding the interpersonal and inner effects of social exclusion. *Social and Personality Compass* 1 (1), 506–520.

Baumeister, R., & Leary, M. (1995). The need to belong: Desire for interpersonal attachments as a fundamental human motivation. *Psychological Bulletin* 117 (3), 497–529.

Bénabou, R., & Tirole, J. (2002). Self-confidence and personal motivation. *The Quarterly Journal of Economics* 117 (3), 871–915.

Benischek, S. A. (1996). *An Inquiry into the Effect of a Management Development Program on Perceived Locus of Control Orientation and Job Satisfaction in Managers and Non-Managers.* (Doctor of Education). University of New Mexico, Albuquerque, New Mexico.

BetterUp. (2017). *Meaning and purpose at work.* Retrieved from https://get.betterup.co/rs/600-WTC-654/images/betterup-meaning-purpose-at-work.pdf.

Biggerstaff, L., Cicero, D. C., & Puckett, A. (2017). Fore! An analysis of CEO shirking. *Management Science* 63 (7), 2049–2395.

Binetti, N., Harrison, C., Coutrot, A., Johnston, A., & Mareschal, I. (2016). Pupil dilation as an index of preferred mutual gaze duration. *Royal Society Open Science.* doi:10.1098/rsos.160086.

Böckerman, P., & Ilmakunnas, P. (2012). The job satisfaction-productivity nexus: A study using matched survey and register data. *Industrial & Labor Relations Review* 65 (2), 244–262.

Brockner, J. (1990). Scope of justice in the workplace: How survivors react to co-worker layoffs. *Journal of Social Issues* 46 (1), 95–106.

Burgard, S. A., Brand, J. E., & House, J. S. (2007). Toward a better estimation of the effect of job loss on health. *Journal of Health and Social Behavior* 48 (December), 369–384.

Cacioppe, R. L. (2017). Integral mindflow: A process of mindfulness-in-flow to enhance individual and organization learning. *The Learning Organization* 24 (6), 408–417.

Cahill, L. (2006). Why sex matters for neuroscience. *Nature Reviews Neuroscience* 7, 477–485.

Caldart, A. A., & Ricart, J. E. (2004). Corporate strategy revisited: a view from complexity theory. *European Management Review* 1 (1), 96–104.

Carlzon, J. (1989). *Moments of truth.* New York: HarperBusiness.

Chowdhury, S. E., Endres, M. E., & Lanis, T. W. (2002). Preparing students for success in team work environments: The importance of building confidence. *Journal of Managerial Issues* 14 (3), 346.

Christakis, N. A., & Fowler, J. H. (2007). The spread of obesity in a large social network over 32 years. *New England Journal of Medicine* 357, 370–379.

Christakis, N. A., & Fowler, J. H. (2008). The collective dynamics of smoking in a large social network. *New England Journal of Medicine* 358, 2249–2258.

Cole, S., Kanz, M., & Klapper, L. (2012). *Incentivizing calculated risk-taking: Evidence from an experiment with commercial bank loan officers*. Retrieved from https://www.hbs.edu/faculty/Publication%20Files/13-002_25637a6c-6de3-4c52-8b3a-ee862f00f5ab.pdf.

Colquhoun, R. J., Gai, C. M., Aguilar, D., Bove, D., Dolan, J., Vargas, A., … Campbell, B. I. (2018). Training volume, not frequency, indicative of maximal strength adaptations to resistance training. *The Journal of Strength & Conditioning Research* 32 (5), 1207–1213.

Csikszentmihalyi, M. (1990). *Flow: The psychology of optimal experience*. New York: Harper & Row.

Davidson, R., Kabat-Zinn, J., Schumacher, J., Rosenkranz, M., Muller, D., Santorelli, S., … Sheridan, J. (2003). Alterations in brain and immune function produced by mindfulness meditation. *Psychosom Medicine* 65 (4), 564–570.

Dolezal, B. A., Neufeld, E. V., Boland, D. M., Martin, J. L., & Cooper, C. B. (2017). Interrelationship between sleep and exercise: A systematic review. *Advances in Preventive Medicine*. doi:10.1155/2017/1364387.

Domenico, S. I. D., & Ryan, R. M. (2017). The emerging neuroscience of intrinsic motivation: A new frontier in self-determination research. *Frontiers in Human Neuroscience* 11 (145), 1–14.

Emond, A., & Eduljee, N. B. (2014). Gender differences: What we seek in romantic and sexual partners. *Universal Journal of Psychology* 2 (2), 90–94.

Fowler, J. H., & Christakis, N. A. (2008). Dynamic spread of happiness in a large social network: Longitudinal analysis over 20 years in the Framingham Heart Study. *British Journal of Management* 337, 2338.

Fuller, R. B. (1981). *Critical path*. New York: St. Martin's Press.

Gallo, W. T., Bradley, E. H., & Falba, T. A. (2004). Involuntary job loss as a risk factor for subsequent myocardial infarction and stroke: Findings from the Health and Retirement Survey. *American Journal of Industrial Medicine* 45 (5), 408–416.

Gallo, W. T., Teng, H.-M., Falba, T. A., Kasl, S. V., Bradley, E. H., & Krumholz, H. M. (2006). The impact of late career job loss on myocardial infarction and stroke: A 10 year follow up using the Health and Retirement Survey. *Journal of Occupational Environmental Medicine* 63 (10), 683–687.

Garcy, A. M., & Vågerö, D. (2013). Unemployment and suicide during and after a deep recession: A longitudinal study of 3.4 million Swedish men and women. *American Journal of Public Health* 103 (6), 1031–1038.

Gelles, D. (2016). *Mindful work*. Boston: Eamon Dolan/Mariner Books.

Gibson, E. (2019). *Results & ROI*. https://www.linkedin.com/pulse/roi-mindfulness-fortune-500s-latest-competitive-edge-gibson-ph-d-/.

Gino, F., & Staats, B. (2015). Why organizations don't learn. *Harvard Business Review* (November). Retrieved from https://search.proquest.com/docview/1746597633?accountid=150425.

Gladwell, M. (producer). (2017, October 15, 2019). *My Little Hundred Million episode of Malcolm Gladwell's Revisionist History podcast* [podcast]. Retrieved from http://revisionisthistory.com/seasons.

Glaser, J. E. (2014). *Conversational intelligence: How great leaders build trust and get extraordinary results*. Brookline, MA: Bibliomotion.

Gomes, G. K., Franco, C. M., Nunes, P. R., & Orsatti, F. L. (2019). High-frequency resistance training is not more effective than low-frequency resistance training in increasing muscle mass and strength in well-trained men. *The Journal of Strength & Conditioning Research* 33, S130–S139.

Gubler, T., Larkin, I., & Pierce, L. (2016). Motivational spillovers from awards: Crowding out in a multitasking environment. *Organization Science* 27 (2), 286–303.

Hafenbrack, A. C., Kinias, Z., & Barsade, S. G. (2014). Debiasing the mind through meditation: Mindfulness and the sunk-cost bias. *Psychological Science* 25 (2), 369–376.

Hamrick, P., Lum, J. A. G., & Ullman, M. T. (2018). *Child first language and adult second language are both tied to general-purpose learning systems*. Paper presented at the Proceedings of the National Academy of Sciences. PNA, 115 (7) 1487–1492.

Handy, L. (1998). *The Ashridge management index.* Ashbridge: Ashridge Management College.

Hollenbeck, G., & Hall, D. (2004). Self-confidence and Leader Performance. *Organizational Dynamics* 33 (3), 254–269.

Horne, J. (2007). *Sleepfaring: The secrets and science of a good night's sleep.* London: Oxford University Press.

Ingalhalikar, M., Smith, A., Parker, D., Satterthwaite, T. D., Elliott, M. A., Ruparel, K., ... Verma, R. (2014). Sex differences in the structural connectome of the human brain. *Proceedings of the National Academy of Sciences of the USA* 111, 823–828.

Kahn, D. (1996). *The codebreakers: The story of secret writing.* New York: Scribner.

Kaplan, R. S., & Norton, D. P. (1992). The Balanced scorecard: Measures that drive performance. *Harvard Business Review* (January–February), 71–79.

Karren, R. (2012). Introduction to the special issue on job loss. *Journal of Managerial Psychology* 27 (8), 772–779.

Kasl, S., & Jones, B. (2000). The impact of job loss and retirement on health. In *Social epidemiology,* edited by L. F. Berkman & I. Kawachi. New York: Oxford University Press.

Kellerman, J., Lewis, J., & Laird, J. D. (1989). Looking and loving: The effects of mutual gaze on feelings of romantic love. *Journal of Research in Personality* 23 (2), 145–161.

Kilduff, G. J. (2014). Driven to win: Rivalry, motivation, and performance. *Social Psychological and Personality Science* 5, 944–952.

Killingsworth, M., & Gilbert, D. (2010). A wandering mind is an unhappy mind. *Science* 330 (6006), 932.

Klucken, T., Tabbert, K., Schweckendiek, J., Merz, C. J., Kagerer, S., Vaitl, D., & Stark, R. (2009). Contingency learning in human fear conditioning involves the ventral striatum. *Human Brain Mapping* 30, 3636–3644.

Knox, B. M. W., Bowersock, G. W., & Burkert, W. (1979). Arktouros: Hellenic studies presented to Bernard M. W. Knox on the occasion of his 65th birthday (pp. 253–255). New York: Walter de Gruyter.

Koike, T., Tanabe, H. C., Okazaki, S., Nakagawa, E., Sasaki, A. T., Shimada, K., ... Sadato, N. (2015). Neural substrates of shared attention as social memory: A hyperscanning functional magnetic resonance imaging study. *Neuroimage* January (125), 401–412.

Kotler, S. (2014). *The rise of superman: Decoding the science of ultimate human performance.* New York: New Harvest.

Kotler, S. (2018). Retrieved from https://www.stevenkotler.com/rabbithole/ea-ullam-copy.

Kozlowski, S., Chao, G., Smith, E., & Hedlund, J. (1993). Organizational downsizing: Strategies, interventions, and research implications. In *International review of industrial and organizational psychology*, edited by C. L. Cooper & I. T. Robertson (pp. 263–332). New York: John Wiley and Sons.

Krasz, K. (2005). Outcomes of redundancy—Different aspects. *Periodica Polytechnica Social and Management Sciences* 13 (1), 61–75.

Larkin, L., & Pierce, F. G. (2012). The psychological costs of pay-for-performance: Implications for the strategic compensation of employees. *Strategic Management Journal* 33 (10), 1194–1214.

Levin, M. (2017). *Why Google, Nike, and Apple love mindfulness training, and how you can easily love it too.* Retrieved from https://www.inc.com/marissa-levin/why-google-nike-and-apple-love-mindfulness-training-and-how-you-can-easily-love-.html.

Limbach, P., & Sonnenburg, F. (2015). *Does CEO fitness matter?* Retrieved from Cologne.

Luthans, F. (2002). The need for and meaning of positive organizational behavior. *Journal of Organizational Behavior* 23 (6), 695.

Luthans, F., Avolio, B. J., Avey, J. B., & Norman, S. M. (2007). *Positive psychological capital: Measurement and relationship with performance and satisfaction.* Retrieved from http://digitalcommons.unl.edu/cgi/viewcontent.cgi?article=1010&context=leadershipfacpub.

Luthans, F., Vogelgesang, G. R., & Lester, P. B. (2006). Developing the psychological capital of resiliency. *Human Resource Development Review* 5 (1), 25.

Macdonald, K., & Macdonald, T. M. (2010). The peptide that binds: A systematic review of oxytocin and its prosocial effects in humans. *Harvard Review of Psychiatry* 18 (1), 1–21.

Madden, T. J. (2015). *Surviving a workforce reduction: Employee attitudes and behaviors that enhance organizational outcomes.* University of Maryland University College. Berwyn, MD.

Mark, G., Gudith, D., & Klocke, U. (2008). *The cost of interrupted work: More speed and stress.* Paper presented at the SIGCHI Conference on Human Factors in Computing Systems, New York.

Mark, G., Iqbal, S., Czerwinski, M., Johns, P., & Sano, A. (2016). *Neurotics can't focus: In Situ of online multitasking in the workplace.* Paper presented at the CHI Conference on Human Factors in Computing Systems. Retrieved from https://www.research-gate.net/publication/301931493_Neurotics_Can't_Focus_An_in_situ_Study_of_Online_Multitasking_in_the_Workplace.

Mindvalley. (producer). (September 15, 2019). *How to get into the flow state* [video]. Retrieved from https://www.youtube.com/watch?v=XG_hNZ5T4nY.

Mintzberg, H. (2013). *Simply managing: What managers do and can do better.* San Francisco: Berrett-Koehler.

Morris, D. (1967). *The naked ape: A zoologist's study of the human animal* (6th ed.). London: Cape.

Murray, B. (2015). More for less: Getting the best performance for the least monetary outlay. *Effective Executive* 18 (1), 13–18.

Neely, A. D., Adams, C., & Kennerley, M. (2002). *The performance prism: The scorecard for measuring and managing stakeholder relationships.* London: Prentice Hall.

Neumann, I. D. (2007). Oxytocin: The neuropeptide of love reveals some of its secrets. *Cell Metabolism* 5 (April), 231–233.

Noelke, C., & Beckfield, J. (2014). Recessions, job loss, and mortality among older US adults. *American Journal of Public Health* 104 (11), 126–134.

Ober, J. (2015). *The rise and fall of classical Greece.* Princeton, NJ: Princeton University Press.

Oppland, M. (2019). *8 Ways to create flow according to Mihaly Csikszentmihalyi.* Retrieved from https://positivepsychology.com/mihaly-csikszentmihalyi-father-of-flow/.

Ortigue, S., Bianchi-Demicheli, F., Patel, N., Frum, C., & Lewis, J. W. (2010). Neuroimaging of love: MRI meta-analysis evidence toward new perspectives in sexual medicine. *Journal of Sexual Medicine* 7 (11), 3541–3552.

Parker, K. J. O. O., Libove, R. A., Sumiyoshi, R. D., Jackson, L. P., Karhson, D. S., Summers, J. E., ... Hardan, A. Y. (2017). *Intranasal oxytocin treatment for social deficits and biomarkers of response in children with autism.* Paper presented at the Proceedings of the National Academy of Sciences. Retrieved from https://eurekamag.com/research/066/424/066424734.php.

Paulsen, A. M., & Betz, N. E. (2004). Basic confidence predictors of career decision-making self-efficacy. *The Career Development Quarterly* 52 (4), 354.

Peper, J. S., & Koolschijn, P. C. (2012). Sex steroids and the organization of the human brain. *The Journal of Neuroscience* 32, 6745–6746.

Pinker, S. (2011). *The better angels of our nature: Why violence has declined.* New York: Viking.

Plutarch. (1914). *The parallel lives.* Loeb Classical Library.

Popper, M., & Mayseless, O. (2007). The building blocks of leader development: A psychological conceptual framework. *Leadership & Organization Development Journal* 28 (7), 664–684.

Razmi, B., & Ghasemi, H. M. (2015). Designing a model of organizational agility: A case study of Ardabil Gas Company. *International Journal of Organizational Leadership* 4 (2), 100–117.

Reilly, A. H., Brett, J. M., & Stroh, L. K. (1993). The impact of corporate turbulence on employee attitudes. *Strategic Management Journal* 14, 167–179.

Riedl, R., & Javor, A. (2012). The biology of trust: Integrating evidence from genetics, endocrinology and functional brain imaging. *Journal of Neuroscience, Psychology, and Economics* 5, 63–91.

Robbins, M. (2017). *The 5 second rule: Transform your life, work, and confidence with everyday courage.* US: Savio Republic.

Robinson, S. (producer). (2012). *Bring back the 40-hour work week*. Retrieved from https://www.salon.com/test/2012/03/14/ bring_back_the_40_hour_work_week/.

Rotter, J. B. (1966). Generalized expectancies for internal versus external control of reinforcement. *Psychological Monographs* 80 (1), 1–28.

Ruef, M. (1997). Assessing organizational fitness on a dynamic landscape: An empirical test of the relative inertia thesis. *Strategic Management Journal* 18 (11), 837–853.

Ryan, L. V. (2017). Sex differences through a neuroscience lens: Implications for business ethics. *Journal of Business Ethics* 144, 771–782.

Sandle, T. (2018). Op-Ed: Knowledge doubles almost every day, and it's set to increase. *Digital Journal*. Retrieved from http://www. digitaljournal.com/tech-and-science/science/op-ed-knowledge- doubles-almost-every-day-and-it-s-set-to-increase/article/537543.

Sawyer, K. (2017). *Group genius: The creative power of collabo- ration* (2nd ed.). New York: Basic Books.

Scheele, D., Striepens, N., Güntürkün, O., Deutschländer, S., Maier, W., Kendrick, K. M., & Hurlemann, R. (2012). Oxytocin modulates social distance between males and females. *Journal of Neuroscience* 32 (46), 16074–16079.

Schneiderman, I., Zagoory-Sharon, O., Leckman, J. F., & Feldman, R. (2012). Oxytocin during the initial stages of romantic attachment: Relations to couples' interactive reciprocity. *Psychoneuroendocrinology* 37 (8), 1277–1285.

Schuh, S. C., Zheng, M. X., Xin, K. R., & Fernandez, J. A. (2019). The interpersonal benefits of leader mindfulness: A serial mediation model linking leader mindfulness, leader procedural justice enactment, and employee exhaustion and performance. *Journal of Business Ethics* 156, 1007–1025.

Seligman, M. (2002). *Authentic happiness: Using the new positive psychology to realize your potential for lasting fulfillment.* New York: Free Press.

Senju, A., & Johnson, M. H. (2009). The eye contact effect: Mechanisms and development. *Trends in Cognitive Science* 13 (3), 127–134.

Siegel, M., Bradley, E., Gallo, W., & Kasl, S. (2003). Impact of husbands' involuntary job loss on wives' mental health, among older adults. *The Journals of Gerontology, Series B, Psychological Sciences and Social Sciences* 58.

Silver, S. (producer). (2018). August 6, 1997—The day Apple and Microsoft made peace. *AppleInsider.* Retrieved from https://appleinsider.com/articles/18/08/06/august-6-1997----the-day-apple-and-microsoft-made-peace.

Smith, M., & Vickers, T. (1994). What about the survivors? *Training and Development* 12 (1), 11–13.

Sportstar. (producer). (October 17, 2019). Ronaldo: Messi "made me better player." Retrieved from https://sportstar.thehindu.com/football/ronaldo-messi-made-me-a-better-player-comments-rivalry-real-madrid-barcelona-juventus-ballon-dor-la-liga-serie-a/article29219719.ece.

Stewart, G. L., Courtright, S. H., & Barrick, M. R. (2012). Peer-based control in self-managing teams: Linking rational and normative influence with individual and group performance. *Journal of Applied Psychology* 97 (2), 435–447.

TIME. (1997). Exclusive: Inside the Microsoft-Apple Deal. *TIME* (August 16, 1997), cover.

Treadway, M. T., Buckholtz, J. W., Cowan, R. L., Woodward, N. D., Li, R., Ansari, M. S., … Zald, D. H. (2012). Dopaminergic mechanisms of individual differences in human effort-based decision-making. *Journal of Neuroscience* 32 (18), 6170–6176.

Van der Stede, W. A., Wu, A., & Wu, S. Y. (2016). *An empirical analysis of employee responses to bonuses and penalties.* Retrieved from https://coller.tau.ac.il/sites/coller-english.tau.ac.il/files/media_server/Recanati/management/conferences/accounting/2018/pdf/wim-van-der-stede.pdf.

Voelpel, S. C., Leibold, M., & Mahmoud, K. M. (2004). The organi zational fitness navigator: Enabling and measuring organizational fitness for rapid change. *Journal of Change Management* 4 (2), 123–140.

Vroom, V. H. (1964). *Work and motivation*. Oxford: Wiley.

Whitmore, J. (2009). *Coaching for performance: The principles and practices of coaching and leadership*. London: Hodder & Stoughton General Division.

Wolever, R., Bobinet, K., McCabe, K., Mackenzie, E., Fekete, E., Kusnick, C., & Baime, M. (2012). Effective and viable mind-body stress reduction in the workplace: A randomized controlled trial. *Journal of Occupational Health Psychology* 17 (2), 246–258.

Worrall, L., Campbell, F., & Cooper, C. (2000). Surviving redundancy: The perceptions of UK managers. *Journal of Managerial Psychology* 15 (5), 460–476.

Wudarczyk, O. A., Earp, B. D., Guastella, A., & Savulescu, J. (2013). Could intranasal oxytocin be used to enhance relationships? Research imperatives, clinical policy, and ethical considerations. *Current Opinion in Psychiatry* 26 (5), 474–484.

Xie, L., Kang, H., Xu, Q., Chen, M. J., Liao, Y., Thiyagarajan, M., ... Nedergaard, M. (2013). Sleep drives metabolite clearance from the adult brain. *Science* 342 (6156), 373–377.

Yang, Y., Bay, P. B., Wang, Y. R., Huang, J., Teo, H. W. J., & Goh, J. (2018). Effects of consecutive versus non-consecutive days of resistance training on strength, body composition, and red blood cells. *Frontiers in Physiology* 9, 725.

Zak, P. J., Boria, K., Matzner, W. T., & Kurzban, R. (2005). The neuroeconomics of distrust: Sex differences in behavior and physiology. *American Economic Review* 95, 360–363.

Zak, P. J., Stanton, A. A., & Ahmadi, S. (2007). Oxytocin increases generosity in humans. *PLoS One* 2 (11), e1128.